THE D
OF CHARTISM

THE DIGNITY OF CHARTISM: ESSAYS BY DOROTHY THOMPSON

Edited by Stephen Roberts

VERSO

London • New York

First published by Verso 2015
© Dorothy Thompson 2015
Introduction and prefaces © Stephen Roberts 2015

The publisher and editor gratefully acknowledge the journals that published earlier versions of the essays collected here: *Amateur Historian*, *Bulletin of the Society for the Study of Labour History*, *Cycnos*, the Encyclopedia of the 1848 Revolutions, *History Workshop Journal*, *Irish Democrat*, *Labour History Review*, *New Reasoner*, *Times Higher Education* and *Times Literary Supplement*. The date and place of original publication are acknowledged in a footnote at the start of each chapter.

1 3 5 7 9 10 8 6 4 2

Verso
UK: 6 Meard Street, London W1F 0EG
US: 20 Jay Street, Suite 1010, Brooklyn, NY 11201

www.versobooks.com

Verso is the imprint of New Left Books

ISBN-13: 978-1-78168-849-6 (PB)
ISBN-13: 978-1-78168-848-9 (HB)
eISBN-13: 978-1-78168-851-9 (US)
eISBN-13: 978-1-78168-850-2 (UK)

British Library Cataloguing in Publication Data
A catalogue record for this book is available from the British Library

The Library of Congress Cataloging-in-Publication Data

Thompson, Dorothy, 1923–2011.
[Essays. Selections]
The dignity of chartism : essays by Dorothy Thompson / edited by Stephen Roberts.
pages cm
ISBN 978-1-78168-849-6 (pbk. : alk. paper) – ISBN 978-1-78168-848-9 (hardback : alk. paper)
1. Chartism – History. 2. Labor movement – Great Britain – History. 3. Working-class – Great Britain –History. I. Roberts, Stephen. II. Title.
HD8396.T452 2015
322ʹ.20941 – dc23
2014043269

Typeset in Sabon by Hewer Text UK Ltd, Edinburgh
Printed and bound by CPI Group (UK) Ltd, Croydon, CR0 4YY

To the memory of Charlie Williams

CONTENTS

PART III. THE LEADERS OF THE PEOPLE

PART IV. REPERCUSSIONS

PART V. LOOKING BACK

ACKNOWLEDGEMENTS

I am indebted to Kate Thompson, who gave permission for the work of her parents to be collected together in this volume and who also patiently answered my numerous requests for assistance. Ben and Mark Thompson both read the introduction, and gave me great help with points of detail. At the outset Kate Tiller discussed this project with me over lunch in Oxford, and, as it came together, offered advice and assistance. Owen Ashton, on several occasions, talked over my plan of action, and also read one section of the book. Bob Fyson, Robert Hall and Ted Royle agreed to read the other sections of the book, and their feedback was much appreciated. I am grateful to Sheila Rowbotham, with whom I enjoyed two long conversations – one in a black cab and the other on a train – about Dorothy and Edward Thompson. I have also profitably discussed sections of this book with Terry Brotherstone, John McIlroy and Malcolm Chase. In their different ways Penny Corfield, Jim Epstein, Julian Harber, Patrick Joyce, Bob Knecht and Bryan D. Palmer have been most supportive. Richard Brown, Margot Finn, John Hargreaves, Antony Taylor, Alex Tyrrell and Cal Winslow responded helpfully to my queries. I am very grateful to Debbie Roberts and Staffordshire University Library for the help and support I received. Pete Bounous and Lewis Jones provided essential technical assistance. My thanks, too, to Sebastian Budgen and Mark Martin at Verso for their expert advice and for reassurance when it was needed.

I would like to acknowledge the support of a number of people who helped clear the way and enabled all of this work to appear between the covers of one volume: Paul Corthorn; Malcolm Chase; Kevin Towndrow; James Chastain; Karen Shook; Alan Crosby and the British Association for Local History; Michael Carty; Terry Brotherstone, Anna Clark and Kevin Whelan; Peter Burns; the Editorial Collective of *History Workshop Journal*; and Christian Gutleben. I have indicated the original place of publication in the first footnote of each essay.

This book is dedicated to the memory of my great-uncle, Charlie Williams. He embraced such causes as communism and vegetarianism, and was arrested on a fabricated charge of striking a police officer when local Communists disrupted a meeting in the Central Hall in Birmingham in 1923. His espousal of the Communist cause cost him his job at Cadbury's, and, at the outbreak of war in 1939, he only just managed to get home from the Soviet Union. I waited thirty years to tell Dorothy Thompson his story. It proved to be the final conversation we had.

EDITORIAL NOTE

Dorothy Thompson's essays and reviews on Chartism were published in many different places. My aim in putting together this collection has been to make her miscellaneous writings on this subject easily accessible. Inevitably, in a collection of pieces written over a period of years and for a range of publications, there will be some overlap and some points that are no longer applicable. Consequently, I have made some deletions, though these are not extensive. To help the reader, I have augmented the footnotes, identifying figures mentioned in the essays and pointing to further reading. The unpublished essay on Halifax Chartism was not completely finished or – at more than 30,000 words – edited. To make it a more suitable length for inclusion in this collection, I have condensed some of the more drawn-out passages and quotations as well as reducing the number of footnotes. The original essay can be read on Ben Thompson's website at www.tufsoft.com/pdf/Halifax Chartists.pdf. Except in passages where Edward Thompson features, I have referred to Dorothy Thompson by her surname in this book.

Edward and Dorothy Thompson at home at Wick Episcopi, near Worcester, mid-1980s.

INTRODUCTION
RETHINKING THE CHARTIST
MOVEMENT: DOROTHY
THOMPSON (1923–2011).

BY STEPHEN ROBERTS

Dorothy Thompson was the pre-eminent historian of Chartism.[1] During half a century of research and writing, she singlehandedly changed the way that we view Chartism. From the early 1950s onwards Thompson began to assiduously collect material on the movement – she particularly prized a manuscript volume inscribed by the West Riding Chartist George White with the motto 'Vive La Libertie' – and to fill notebook after notebook with her discoveries and thoughts. In Halifax, Worcester and the University of Birmingham, she generously shared everything with fellow scholars and with the many postgraduate students she so affectionately supervised. Her long-planned book *The Chartists*, delayed as she brought up three children, finally appeared in 1984. Deeply sympathetic, rich in detail, reflective and very readable, the book completely captured the essence of the movement. At the heart of Thompson's Chartist project was the need to rehabilitate Feargus O'Connor. She had been concerned that J. T. Ward's *Chartism* (1973) had accepted at face value the hostile judgements of the Chartist leader made by R. G. Gammage

---

1. This essay was first published in *Labour History Review*, 76:2 (2011), 161–8. This is a revised and extended version.

and William Lovett, and was determined that his talent and drive be recognized. Already, under her influence, James Epstein had published *The Lion of Freedom* (1982), but Thompson's book sought to ensure that Feargus truly was given his historical due; in a well-known sentence, she wrote that 'had the name Chartist not been coined, the radical movement between 1838 and 1848 must surely have been called O'Connorite Radicalism.'[2] To the end of her life Thompson remained a doughty defender of the Irishman; she described him to me as 'one of the most underrated men in history', and Paul Pickering's biography was described – in an honour usually reserved only for the detective novels she devoured – as 'unputdownable'.[3]

Dorothy Katherine Gane Towers was born in Greenwich, south London, on 30 October 1923. It was her paternal grandfather, a shoemaker who worked part-time in music halls, who had settled in the capital. Her parents, Reginald and Katharine, were both professional musicians who met at the Royal Academy of Music, though most of their income came from running shops which sold musical instruments (and later televisions) and teaching. They were both support-ers (but not members) of the Labour Party, and Dorothy and her brothers Tom, Glen and Alan grew up in a household where politics and family history were regularly discussed and where the *Daily Herald* and *Reynolds's News* were taken: she recalled Tom sending the contents of his money box to the miners in 1926. Her brother Tom was not in robust health and so the family moved to Kent, first to the agricultural village of Keston and then to Bromley. In Keston the family lived in a four-room cottage lit by oil lamps and candles, soaked themselves in a zinc bath in front of the fire and visited an outside lavatory that was not at first connected to the mains water supply. 'I could read by the time I was three', Thompson later recalled, 'and cannot remember ever facing a page of print I couldn't understand.' In her first

2. D. Thompson, *The Chartists* (London, 1984), p. 96.
3. P. A. Pickering, *Fergus O'Connor: A Political Life* (Monmouth, 2008).

weeks at school (St. Margaret's, run by two spinsters), Thompson demonstrated her prowess in reading and singing, boarding the slow-moving bus each morning when 'the boy from the garage handed me to the conductor'.[4] Summer holidays were spent either accompanying her mother to visit relations in France, or with her maternal grandmother in Gloucestershire (a phrase Thompson adopted from her grandmother was 'Gloucestershire generosity', meaning to pass on an unwanted gift).

At the age of fourteen, Thompson became politically active, joining the Labour Monthly Discussion Club and, very soon, the Young Communist League. Supported by almost one hundred young people, the Bromley branch of the YCL was a lively and stimulating environment. On Saturday mornings Thompson could be found in the high street selling *Challenge*, and she spent some weekday evenings at YCL headquarters in central London. In the small sixth form of Bromley County Girls' School, Thompson studied history and languages (enjoying one-to-one tuition in Greek and German) and, encouraged by her Oxbridge-educated teachers, developed an ambition to go on to university. With foreign travel ruled out by war and a degree in languages therefore less enticing, Thompson decided to read history. 'Her interests are intellectual and artistic', her head teacher wrote, 'and her intellectual work is . . . good, occasionally brilliant'. Full of life, with interests in the school orchestra, singing, acting, debating and socialising, Thompson did not get the examination results she hoped for; but nevertheless, in October 1942, she arrived at Girton College, Cambridge, as an exhibitioner (worth £30; her LEA added another £110 and her school another £10). Before she went up to Girton, she was asked if she would conceal her party membership and infiltrate other organizations – a proposal she thought ridiculous.[5]

In that early period at Cambridge, before leaving in 1944 to undertake war work as an industrial draughtsperson in

---

4. Autobiographical fragment in the possession of Kate Thompson.
5. Tutorial file, GCAC 2/4/4/49, Archives, Girton College, Cambridge.

London, Thompson met her first husband, Gilbert Buchanan Sale, a student at Pembroke; she later recalled many early mornings making her exit over the college walls. She also fell under the influence of Helen Cam, an expert on medieval local government: Thompson was to remember her as 'a wonderful historian . . . a marvellous person to work with.' Thompson had married Sale in November 1944, but very soon after formed the relationship that would define her life. Edward Thompson had returned from leading a tank troop in Italy to resume his studies at Corpus Christi College, from where he was to graduate with first-class honours in history and English. 'We were both interested in history, both members of the Communist Party', she later recollected. 'I fancied him, he fancied me. I suppose that's all one can say.'[6] (Edward in fact sealed the deal by buying her a recording of Benjamin Britten's 'A Young Person's Guide to the Orchestra'.) Having secured an upper second for her degree, Dorothy began living with Edward until, in 1948, she was able to obtain a divorce.

By this time the Thompsons had spent a lengthy period in the company of many other young left-wing activists of different nationalities in Yugoslavia, helping construct the Samac-Sarajevo Youth Railway. Motivated by a desire to help actually build the new Europe, not just talk about it, they spent each day from six in the morning until midday in hard physical work, breaking rocks and loading and pushing trucks; the rest of the day was spent walking, singing, dancing and talking about history and politics. On their return Edward secured a post teaching in the Department of Extra-Mural Studies at the University of Leeds.[7] The couple set up house in Halifax, a location

---

6. Interview with Sheila Rowbotham, *New Left Review* (July/August 1993), 87–100. Also see Sheila Rowbotham, *Remembering Edward and Dorothy* (Worcester, 2014). Thompson wrote about her own early life in *Outsiders: Class, Gender and Nation* (London, 1993), pp. 1–18. Edward Thompson joined the Communist Party in 1942 and the same year was elected President of the Cambridge University Socialist Club. From 1945 onwards he was contributing regularly to *Our Time*.

7. See P. Searby and editors, 'Edward Thompson as a Teacher:

chosen because it was steeped in Chartist and socialist history (though Dorothy never lost her love of London and its culture). During these years, when nineteenth-century volumes could be picked up cheaply, they began to build up what became a superb library. Though both were members of the Communist Party Historians' Group (CPHG), it was Dorothy who most regularly attended meetings (Edward preferred the literature group and was regularly writing poetry). Thompson's interest in Chartism stretched back to her time in the sixth form, and at Cambridge she had protested about its absence from the syllabus. In September 1950 she formalized this interest by registering as a postgraduate student at the University of Leeds. It was her intention to work, under Asa Briggs's supervision, on Ernest Jones and late Chartism, an area she considered greatly neglected.[8]

Though little progress was ever to be made in writing the thesis, Thompson was beginning to appear in print on the subject of Chartism. She contributed a two-page article on the poets and poetry of the movement to a Chartist-themed edition of the Communist Party of Great Britain (CPGB) journal *Our Time* in April 1948, and a sympathetic piece on O'Connor to the *Irish Democrat* in September 1952. In offering a scholarly evaluation of Chartist poetry, Thompson was breaking new ground. She was impressed by the authenticity of this verse. 'Shelley's *Song to the Men of England*', she wrote, 'pales into romantic word-spinning beside the best of these Chartist hymns and anthems.' She supported this argument with some deft extracts, including this portrayal of the Liberal factory owner:

> Against the slave trade he had voted,
> 'Rights of Man' resounding still;

Yorkshire and Warwick', in J. Rule and R. Malcolmson, eds, *Protest and Survival: Essays for E. P. Thompson* (London, 1993), pp. 1–23, for a first-rate account of Edward's work in adult education.

8.   University of Leeds, Brotherton Library Special Collections, History Department Files (Professor A.J. Taylor), Box A2 (miscellaneous to 1965). I am grateful to Malcolm Chase for this reference.

> Now, basely turning, brazen-throated,
> Yelled against the Ten Hours Bill.[9]

Thompson's interest in artisan poetry was to wane – any real discussion is noticeably absent from *The Chartists*. Her fascination with Jones, however, continued to grow, and there were many conversations with John Saville, both in Halifax and at meetings of the CPHG. Saville was laboriously transcribing Jones's writings for an anthology – whilst Thompson fully expected to get round to writing a full biography.[10] At this time she also began collecting original prints of the Chartists; her print of John Frost arrived glued to a Christmas card in 1950.

Holly Bank, the house where the Thompsons lived for seventeen years in Halifax, was a family home (Ben was born in 1948, Mark in 1951 and Kate in 1956), but also an operations centre for historical research and political discussion and activity.[11] It was invariably full of people, debating and arguing about the working people of the past and the politics of the Communist Party and the fledgling peace movement; a number of short-lived political papers emerged from this frenzy of activity, most famously, from 1957 until 1960, the *New Reasoner*. Visitors and several cats were fed and typewriter ribbons bought from Edward's income (initially £425) as a full-time adult education tutor of history and literature, and Dorothy's much smaller part-time income in the same capacity, and also as an interviewer for university-based sociological enquiries; some extra help came from both sets of parents. There was writing to be done – Edward sometimes remaining in his study all day and through the night – and so the garden was rarely

---

9. D. Towers, 'The Chartist Poets', *Our Time* (April 1948), 168–9.

10. J. Saville, ed., *Ernest Jones, Chartist* (London, 1952), p. 9; J. Saville, *Memoirs from the Left* (London, 2003), pp. 86, 104; M. Chase, 'The Chartist Movement and 1848', in D. Howell, D. Kirby and K. Morgan, eds, *John Saville: Commitment and History* (London, 2011), pp. 156–8.

11. Kate Thompson is an award-winning writer, principally of children's fiction. Her mother would observe with pride that she had more books in print than both of her parents put together.

tended, and cleaning, washing and cooking were undertaken by local women. (At Wick Episcopi in Worcester,
Beryl and Manny Ruehl helped Edward tend the garden at
weekends and Dorothy, even after she lived alone at
Rainbow Hill, continued to employ a housekeeper.) These
years in Halifax were extremely happy for the Thompsons;
not only were three children born (looked after for several
weeks each year by Edward so that Dorothy could spend
time working in archives and libraries in London), but two
books appeared from Edward's pen: *William Morris* (1955)
and his hugely influential *The Making of the English
Working Class* (1963), drawing in part on his wife's notes
and discussed step-by-step with her. If a study of Chartism
might have seemed a natural sequel, that was a book that
was never going to come – Edward did not wish to tread on
his wife's toes.

Dorothy and Edward Thompson were considerable
admirers of Dona Torr, who in 1946 had set up the CPHG.
The grand old lady of Communist Party politics, Torr also
shared Dorothy's love for music and languages: she had
translated a German edition of the letters of Marx and
Engels. Whenever Thompson was in London, she met up
with Torr. 'On at least one occasion,' Thompson later
recalled, 'I became so involved in discussion with her that we
missed our stop on the underground and had returned to
central London before we realized that we had been to
Stanmore and back.'[12] If Thompson ever had a political hero
or heroine, it was undoubtedly Dona Torr. Though neither
she nor Edward, who was putting the finishing touches to his
biography of William Morris, were able to contribute to a
festschrift published in honour of Torr at this time, they had
embarked on a collaboration to investigate working-class
politics in Halifax in the pre-Chartist and Chartist period.
The long, jointly-written essay which eventually emerged
from this research did not, in the end, appear in the volume
for which it was intended, Asa Briggs's *Chartist Studies*
(1959). It is published in this collection for the first time.

---

12. Thompson, *Outsiders*, p. 11.

Locally, Thompson made an impact as a political activist; in the late 1940s she organized campaigns in the West Riding to keep wartime nurseries open. Just as she had in Bromley, she sold Communist Party literature in the open air – though, she later recalled, the experience taught her never to impose her own values on working people: one woman told her she only bought the publications because Edward seemed such a nice young man! It was not just the dangers of the atom bomb that the Thompsons spoke out about in these years; they were also very concerned about the brutal suppression of the Mau Mau rebellion in Kenya.[13] Though she felt the deepest attachment to the Communist Party and never forgot the opportunities it gave her in life, Thompson was in truth somewhat difficult for the party hierarchy to manage. Never one to simply do as she was told, she spoke her mind and blazing rows ensued. In a few typed and duplicated sheets, on which they bestowed the same title as G. J. Holyoake's famous Victorian radical journal, the Thompsons called on the Communist Party to tolerate dissenting opinions. The three issues of the *Reasoner* that came out in 1956 prepared them, of course, for their dramatic break from the Communist Party. They must have known that their dissent would lead to suspension or expulsion; but Dorothy claimed that neither of them actually discussed leaving the Communist Party until each had independently decided to do so. In Dorothy's case it was after a discussion at a meeting of the CPHG in London, following Khrushchev's famous speech. That evening she telephoned Edward, who had been attending a Party meeting in Yorkshire, and was very relieved to discover that he had reached the same decision. Leaving the Communist Party, she later wrote, was 'very liberating . . . I became a member of what we used to describe as the biggest party in the country, the ex-party.'[14]

---

13. I am grateful to Ted Royle for this information. Edward Thompson edited the *Yorkshire Voice of Peace* at this time.

14. Unpublished paper on the Communist Party in the possession of S. Roberts. In 1956–57 some 7,000 people – over a quarter of the membership – turned their backs on the Communist Party.

A few days before Dorothy Thompson left Wick Episcopi in Worcester in July 1997, I managed to salvage a few copies of the *New Reasoner* which were scattered across the floors of the attics. Though designated business manager of the journal, Dorothy was in effect a co-editor with Edward and John Saville, reading all the submissions and also contributing herself, on both history and the efforts to create a new left in the late half of the 1950s. In its pages she welcomed the publication of A. R. Schoyen's study of Julian Harney as 'the first important work on the Chartist Movement' and called for the abandonment of 'moralizing and lesson-drawing . . . [and] instead deep research into the facts'. Elsewhere we find Thompson reporting from a conference of the French Left she attended in Lyon in autumn 1958 with delegates from across Europe; though she thoroughly enjoyed the debates, which lasted from nine o'clock until midnight, she was not optimistic about the prospects of the French Communist Party.[15] By this time the Thompsons had both joined the Labour Party. Since they were known for recruiting Labour Party activists into the ranks of the Communist Party, their applications had gone all the way to the National Executive Committee. On the grounds that the constituency party lacked intellectuals, their applications were accepted. Thompson was in the running to become Labour Party candidate for Halifax for the 1959 election, but in the event Peter Shore was selected and only narrowly defeated.[16] The couple's membership of the Labour Party proved to be short-lived (though it was briefly revived in the early 1980s), but Dorothy always believed that those who wrote about Chartism better understood the movement if they were also involved in the political campaigns of their own times.

---

15. *New Reasoner* 8 (Spring 1959), 139–41; ibid. 7 (Winter 1958–59), 108–111.

16. I am grateful to Julian Harber for this information. The results were: M. Macmillan (Con), 29,212; P. Shore (Lab), 26,697. The Thompsons got on well with Shore and were disappointed when he changed his mind about unilateral nuclear disarmament in the 1980s.

In the wake of the huge impact of *The Making*, Edward received an offer that meant both giving up adult education and leaving the West Riding; but, with the opportunity to instigate, encourage and influence so much research into working-class history, it was an offer that could not be turned down. And so in 1965 Edward took up the post of director of the Centre for the Study of Social History at the University of Warwick. The family moved to Lansdowne Crescent in Leamington Spa, and in 1971 to Wick Episcopi near Worcester. Dorothy attended many of the fortnightly seminars organized by Edward, and continued with her part-time work; in 1961–63 she had been employed by Saville as a researcher for the *Dictionary of Labour Biography*, and afterwards accepted an invitation to write a school textbook.[17] But the time was coming when she felt ready to obtain full-time work in a university department. In 1970, after two years as a research fellow, she was appointed a full-time lecturer in modern history at the University of Birmingham. Liked by her students, she remained in the School of History until 1988, teaching in a part-time capacity in her final few years. Penny Corfield, who held a temporary post in the department, remembered their time together with great affection:

> The University was never an ultra-fashionable one. But that suited Dorothy . . . The calm authority of Birmingham as a well-established civic redbrick matched her own cool style . . . She was a superb role model as the up-to-date female academic: a feminist with charm, intelligence, commitment, tenacity, a streak of combativeness and a lively sense of humour. As joint beginners there, we were both amused and amazed at the micro-politics of academia. People were unofficially grouped into friends or foes according to intricate disputes, both academic and political, that dated from years previously. We newcomers were pre-allocated into the left(ish)-wing team, who were nice to us. So it took some months to find that not all our official

17. D. Thompson, *The British People 1760–1902* (London, 1969).

friends were heroes and, simultaneously, that some of the right(ish)-wing enemies were really quite decent chaps. Dorothy, who within Edward had lived through bruising arguments within the Communist Party and on the post-communist Left, was much less fussed. Indeed, when we discussed these squabbles later, I realized that she rather enjoyed being immersed in a scene that was absorbing without being fundamentalist, although, like all research academics, she became less enchanted with university life as it got ever more bureaucratised .[18]

It was the promise of the publication of a substantial collection of largely forgotten primary source material that had added weight to Thompson's case for a lecture-ship, and *The Early Chartists* duly appeared in 1971. This anthology, which drew on rare material from her own collection, was the first of its kind.[19] Dealing with the years that most interested Thompson, the volume was completed with an outstanding essay. Students who chose to study her final year special subject on Chartism were all equipped with a copy of the book, until supplies ran out sometime in the early 1980s. This was typical of Thompson's generosity; in the thirty-plus years I knew her, I often carried away from her home, or received in the post, quite a number of Victorian volumes as gifts. In 1978 Thompson collaborated with J. F. C. Harrison in compiling a bibliography of Chartism; unfortunately, neither kept a close eye on the project and the publisher brought out a preliminary version. Dorothy talked of her plans to write a single-volume study of Chartism – and was peeved when J. T. Ward beat her to it – but the book was constantly delayed. This did not help her career

---

18.   P. Corfield, 'Dorothy Thompson and Birmingham', in University of Birmingham, *Friends of the Centre for West Midlands History* 8 (August 2011).

19.   Up until this point there was a section devoted to Chartism in G. D. H. Cole and A. W. Filson, eds, *British Working-Class Movements: Select Documents 1789–1875* (London, 1951) and Y. Kovalev, ed., *An Anthology of Chartist Literature* (Moscow, 1956).

prospects: in the twenty years she was at Birmingham, she was never promoted.

In truth, much as she enjoyed her independent career at Birmingham, it was the discussions that were happening at the family home Wick Episcopi rather than in the School of History that Thompson found most stimulating. The concluding section of Edward's *Whigs and Hunters* (1975), as he admitted, was shaped by vigorous discussion with Dorothy.[20] All of Thompson's postgraduates entered this extraordinary world of scholarly generosity and co-operation. Scholars flowed through Wick with their latest drafts to discuss or with news of an interesting archival find. The Thompsons ensured that every visitor felt she had something to contribute in the great collective effort to recover the stories of forgotten working-class men and women. Over lunch, or sipping huge cups of coffee made by that great tea-drinker Edward (which Dorothy never touched until they were almost cold), postgraduate students were guided and encouraged. At the start of each year academics, writers and Dorothy's students invariably found themselves in the music room, reciting poetry or joining in singing; each summer a huge picnic was organized in the garden. It is perhaps not surprising that in this vibrant environment, postgraduate students thrived; many of Thompson's research students have gone on to publish extensively on Chartism and other aspects of working-class history. As well as the great collective effort that the Thompsons oversaw at Wick, there were also invitations to teach abroad: Dorothy spent time at universities in the USA (1975, 1976, 1980–81, 1983, 1989–90) and also in China (1985), Canada (1988) and Japan (1991).

Sometimes Edward felt optimistic about the causes he supported, sometimes he felt anguished, and these shifts, as Penny Corfield has observed, 'must have made [him] hard to live with, at least in the downturns which were often prolonged ... how much Thompson must have gained

---

20. Corfield, 'Dorothy Thompson and Birmingham'. Also see Corfield, Letter: Dorothy Thompson , *Guardian*, 25 February 2011.

from his wife and life-partner's magnificent inner calm. Even Dorothy Thompson, however, did not find it all easy.'[21] It was certainly unwise, as I discovered, to ask Edward about his own historical research in the first half of the 1980s – though his irritation soon melted away. This was at the height of his commitment to the peace movement, and as each pamphlet was published Dorothy put a signed copy in the post to those of her students who supported the cause. Though she put many hours into promoting the peace movement, editing *Over Our Dead Bodies: Women Against the Bomb* (1982), her own academic work also blossomed. With James Epstein, she edited *The Chartist Experience* (1982), which stands amongst half a dozen or so utterly indispensable volumes for the study of Chartism. All of the essays had been thrashed out by the contributors, not on hard chairs in university seminar rooms, but in weekend-long meetings on the comfortable sofas at Wick. The collection had more of a local focus than has perhaps been recognized – over half of the essays examined a particular geographical area – but it did move scholarship on to consider other lines of enquiry, not least Thompson's own discussion of the Irish dimension to Chartism.

Throughout the summers of 1980–83, with notebooks and photocopies strewn across the floor of the guest flat at Wick, Thompson typed furiously in an attempt to get her long-awaited book finished. She had things to say – but she was determined to base every point on deep research into the movement. It was a confusing time for students of Chartism, but, after *The Chartists* finally appeared in 1984, there was a feeling that a few key matters had been set straight: Chartism was a movement with class at its heart, there was a very considerable female presence in the struggle for working-class political rights, and O'Connor, far from being the destructive egotist of earlier accounts, was

---

21. P. Corfield, review of S. Hamilton, *The Crisis of Theory: E. P. Thompson, the New Left and Post-War British Politics* (Manchester, 2011), *Reviews in History* website, www.history.ac.uk/reviews/, 1 September 2011.

the principal architect of this powerful national campaign. In terms of the ways in which it sought to reinterpret the ways we saw the movement, *The Chartists* remains the most significant work written on the subject. Thompson now had the book to show what many had always known – that she was the leading authority in the world on Chartism. The long-awaited book was soon followed by a twenty-two-volume collection of periodicals, pamphlets and autobiographies written by the Chartists; reading these facsimiles, with their erratic typography, was the next best thing to reading the originals.[22] If retirement from teaching was approaching, retirement from scholarship most certainly was not. *Queen Victoria: Gender and Power* (1990) sought to show how the gender of the monarch made republicanism a largely inconspicuous strand of nineteenth-century radicalism. Though relying principally on secondary sources, Thompson approached her subject very differently to earlier biographers of royalty: even if unable to prove it, she clearly thought it likely that Victoria shared more than just a glass of whisky with her servant John Brown. A book on 'Empress Brown' was one she had always known she would write, and she dedicated it to a great-grandmother she remembered and admired – Anne Coleman, born the year Victoria came to the throne into a family of East London silk weavers, who, with the early death of her husband, brought up five children alone. Chartism, however, still stalked Thompson's thoughts, and she was soon preparing a collection of some of her better-known essays on the subject. *Outsiders: Class, Gender and Nation* (1993) was a perfect summation of the issues that she thought mattered if we were to properly understand the movement.

I visited Dorothy and Edward Thompson (or Heathcliff and Mrs Beeton, as one journalist, much to their amusement, described them) at Wick Episcopi regularly throughout the 1980s and into the 1990s. I was there in

---

22. D. Thompson, ed., *Chartism: Working-Class Politics in the Industrial Revolution* (New York, 1986).

August 1991 when hardliners staged a coup in the Soviet Union. The phone rang and Dorothy picked it up. It was the *Guardian*, enquiring what Edward thought about these events. 'Who knows what those bastards in Moscow will do next?' was his only comment; it wasn't printed. In his final years Edward was often hospitalized, but, with Dorothy's support, he carried on writing. He died in August 1993, under his favourite lilac tree in the garden at Wick. In the next few years, requests for help with biographies began to reach Dorothy; she refused to be involved with any of them, declaring that those who wanted to know about Edward had his books to read, and depositing his papers with a fifty-year moratorium in the Bodleian Library (though subsequently she occasionally granted permission for a researcher to examine specific parts of the collection). Thompson in fact was never keen on biographies as a genre. 'I could do a book on the foibles of famous lefties which might be quite a revelation,' she observed. '[But] I don't think that book will get written.'[23] In 1994 Thompson was awarded an honorary doctorate by Staffordshire University, but her own students also felt it was time for them to honour her. So, in January 1996 at the University of Birmingham, she was presented with a festschrift made up of twelve essays. *The Duty of Discontent* took its very apt title from a phrase coined by the Chartist Thomas Cooper; declaring herself to be 'overwhelmed ... an absolutely super book and ... much more than I deserve', she ensured that each of her grandchildren, of whom she was extremely proud, received a copy.[24]

Thompson was never short of suggestions for work that could be done on Chartism. One afternoon, in a discussion with me at Wick, she came up with the idea of a one-day conference and a volume collecting together the contemporary illustrations of the movement. Chartism Day, first held

---

23. D. Thompson to S. Hamilton, 27 January 2011, email reproduced on *Reading the Maps* website http://readingthemaps.blogspot.com/2011/02/last-e-mail-from-dorothy.html
24. D. Thompson to S. Roberts, December 1995.

at the University of Birmingham in 1995, has now become established as an annual event. *Images of Chartism* (1998) brought together eighty pictures, ten of them from the walls of Wick and the rest from a lot of legwork in libraries and record offices across the country. It all amounted to, quite literally, a new way of seeing the Chartists.[25]

Dorothy Thompson relished life. She wrote and argued not only about history and politics (latterly sending money to the Socialist Labour Party), but also greatly enjoyed travel, detective novels, coffee in bed, attending musical performances in London and undertaking work in the garden (at Rainbow Hill she planted a beautiful olive tree in memory of Edward). It was quite easy to spend an entire meal with Thompson discussing nothing but music. I remember once at Wick mentioning Handel's 'I know my redeemer liveth' – and she immediately began to sing it. At Wick, and later at Rainbow Hill, there would be recitals on the square piano by the classical pianist Evy King, or by Thompson's son Ben. But she was only too aware that others did not enjoy such fulfilling lives, and so supported her local credit union with her time and with donations. Though physically frail in her final years, Thompson was fine 'from the eyebrows up' and continued to address the occasional academic gathering. She was very glad to be able to keep in touch with people by email; there could be few octogenarians, she would boast, who made such regular use of this technology. The queries that arrived electronically at Rainbow Hill at this time often related to the CPHG and to Frank Thompson, Edward's brother who was executed in Bulgaria in 1944; these correspondents were doubtless surprised and delighted by the full replies they received.[26]

The essays in this volume make abundantly clear the considerable impact Dorothy Thompson had on the study

---

25. Thompson's collection of prints and artefacts relating to Chartism are now in the People's History Museum in Manchester.

26. Hamilton's *The Crisis of Theory* and P. J. Conradi's *A Very English Hero: The Making of Frank Thompson* (London, 2012) were written with Thompson's support and assistance.

of Chartism. No single scholar spent so many years seeking to rethink the movement. When, in the late 1940s, Thompson first became interested in Chartism and intent on investigating it, she found the existing scholarship unsatisfactory. Living in the old Chartist stronghold of Halifax, she saw the existing histories of the movement as drawing too much on one-sided sources from London, notably the papers of Francis Place. Chartism was not, she reasoned, a movement sustained by London leaders such as Lovett and with O'Connor as its arch-villain in the north (Lovett, she was fond of saying, 'couldn't run a whelk stall'). From the mid-1950s Thompson strongly encouraged local studies, though, as these grew in number, she came to believe that they were tending to obscure the national character of Chartism. It was for this reason that she decided to write a single-volume study of Chartism. With the publication of this book, it was clear that the landscape of Chartist studies had been transformed. O'Connor had been rehabilitated, the potency of Chartism transferred from London to the north, and the role of women and the links with the Irish established. The force of Thompson's influence is made clear in the acknowledgements sections of so many of the books published on Chartism from the mid-1970s onwards.

Dorothy Thompson always spoke her mind. 'You knew where you stood with her,' Bryan D. Palmer noted. 'Dorothy was opinionated,' Joe White recalled. 'But . . . in such a disarming way that defending your position was the last thing you wanted to do. Like the time I was expounding the view that one of America's great gifts to world happiness was frozen, concentrated orange juice. "Nonsense," said Dorothy. And that was that.'[27] Dorothy Thompson was also known for her kindness at times of personal distress, her loyalty and her great generosity with her notes, with her books, with her ideas and with her time. No student she ever taught, ever encouraged, would deny that knowing Thompson, and learning from her, was one of the best

---

27. B. D. Palmer, *History Workshop Journal* 74 (2012), 301; J. White, *Labour History Review* 76:3 (December 2011), 229.

things that had happened to them in all their lives. No one who spent time at Wick Episcopi, eating, laughing, singing, talking and arguing with the people who were so warmly welcomed into that great house, will ever forget those quite wonderful experiences.

I

INTERPRETING CHARTISM

In the first piece in this section, an informal presentation to a conference, Dorothy Thompson reflects on some of the key issues confronting those researching and writing about Chartism – including when it can be said to have begun, its national and local dimensions, its recourse to violence and its legacy. One issue that is not raised is the importance of class. Up until the 'linguistic turn' of the 1980s, there had been no doubt amongst the overwhelming majority of labour historians that the Chartist movement was underpinned by a strong sense of class identity. Thus, Thompson's graduate student James Epstein, in a brilliant review which torpedoed J. T. Ward's narrative history of the movement, was speaking for all of his colleagues when he complained that there was 'almost no sustained treatment of the question of class consciousness ... the scale and intensity of class consciousness and class antagonism during the Chartist years was unparalleled.'[1]

---

1. *Bulletin of the Society for the Study of Labour History* 28 (1974), 68–72. For Epstein's later reflections on these matters see *Radical Expression: Political Language, Ritual and Symbol in England 1790–1850* (Oxford, 1994) and *In Practice: Studies in the Language and Culture of Popular Politics in Modern Britain* (Palo Alto, Calif., 2003). Where Thompson's own thinking had reached at this point is set out in her long

The consciousness of class is certainly not neglected in the two essays which follow. Gareth Stedman Jones, in an essay initially published in *The Chartist Experience* (1982), edited by Epstein and Thompson, and then in a revised and extended version in his own *Languages of Class* (1983), sought to challenge the importance of class in understanding Chartism. In an analysis of Chartist language, he suggested that the movement should be seen as a continuation of political struggles dating back to the late eighteenth century to secure reform of a corrupt state, and not as a distinctly class movement. 'It came out at a very strategic moment,' Epstein later recalled. 'Not sure Gareth even realized how the piece would catch the academic wind.'[2] Thompson expected the interest in the essay to die down. However, the debate persisted, and she could no longer remain silent. The essay she wrote was a persuasive repudiation of Stedman Jones's arguments.

The year 1842 was one of great events in the Chartist struggle – the second petition, signed by 3.3 million working people, was presented and rejected in May, and across the manufacturing districts that July and August a wave of strikes and riots broke out. In an essay focusing on the second petition and relations between the Chartists and the Anti-Corn Law League as ways of defining what was meant by the term 'the people', Thompson sought to demonstrate the validity of the class analysis. The title of her essay clearly alluded to Patrick Joyce's much-talked-about rejection of the class analysis, *Visions of the People* (1991).[3] For Thompson 'the people' were unquestionably

---

review of J. Foster's *Class Struggle and the Industrial Revolution* (London, 1974) in the *Times Literary Review*, 27 September 1974.

2. J. Epstein to S. Roberts, 25 January 2013.

3. D. Thompson to S. Roberts, n.d.: 'Very many thanks for lending me Patrick's book. I was anticipating having to read it in precious BL time, given my absurd prejudice against buying it'; D. Thompson to S. Roberts, 16 March 1993: 'Ulrike [Schwab's] book herewith. You have the better of the exchange, I think – it looks much more interesting than bally old Patrick Joyce's book.'

working-class men, women and children, united by a clear understanding of their own class interests.

At the forefront of Thompson's research was uncovering the role played by women in Chartism. In this area, as in others, she undoubtedly led the way, publishing an important essay in 1976.[4] Previous historians had had very little to say on this issue – J. T. Ward, for example, managed to mention the London tailor Charles Neesom but not his radically-minded wife, Elizabeth.[5] A collection of Thompson's writings could hardly omit this subject, and included here is a little-known contribution to a website. It is a useful summary of her thinking.

The final two essays consider what we can learn about Chartism from the vast number of pamphlets that were put out, often locally, chiefly to explain the case for the Charter but also to comment on such issues as the right to carry arms or the Land Plan, and from the later autobiographies of the participants. The most well-known pamphlets included, from 1840, *The Question 'What is a Chartist?' Answered*, published by the Finsbury Tract Society, and John Taylor's *The Coming Revolution* (which is not as absorbing as the title suggests).[6] These pamphlets are sober, earnest writings which demonstrate mastery of an argument, but lack the vitality and liveliness of the famous *Northern Star*. To know, and to understand, the Chartists, it is imperative to read the *Star*. Though Thompson made use of Benjamin Wilson's memoir in her work on Halifax Chartism, she found that, for the most part, artisan autobiographies were not written by those involved in the northern-based, confrontational side of the

---

4. D. Thompson, 'Women and Nineteenth-Century Radical Politics: A Lost Dimension', in M. Juliet and A. Oakley, eds, *The Rights and Wrongs of Women* (London, 1976) and reprinted in Thompson, *Outsiders*, pp. 77–102.

5. For Elizabeth Neesom see M. Chase, *Chartism* (London, 2006), pp. 184–91.

6. Taylor (1805–42), colourfully attired and very proud of his long hair, was a romantic revolutionary who was very active as a lecturer in the north of England in 1838–40. See W. H. Fraser, *Dr John Taylor, Chartist* (Ayrshire, 2006).

movement that most interested her. Inevitably, in the great celebration of Liberalism in the 1870s and 1880s, it was those who had spurned drilling on the moors in 1839 and 1848 who told their stories.

1

CHARTISM AS AN HISTORICAL SUBJECT

As soon as you begin to define Chartism, there is the problem of separating 'true Chartism' from 'influences'.[1] G. D. H. Cole's method, when he wrote *Chartist Portraits* (1941; reptd. 1989), was to try and illustrate both. Five of the portraits are of men who had a profound influence on the movement, although they were not actually Chartists, and the other seven were of the most articulate leaders. *Chartist Studies* (1959), edited by Asa Briggs, tackled the problem differently, by showing the varying trends at work in particular areas. Both books were to some extent a reaction against earlier attempts to see Chartism as a body of doctrine, or the development of a consistent political system and programme. A subsequent approach was the 'series of responses' type of definition, which saw the movement chiefly as 'protest'. Just as stressing local differences can result in losing sight of what was one of the most significant facts of the movement – its national character – so the 'protest' view can lead to a suggestion of spontaneity and

---

1. This essay was first published in *Bulletin of the Society of Labour History* 20 (Spring 1970), 10–13. This is a slightly shortened version. D. Thompson, 'Chartism, Success or Failure?' in D. Rubenstein, ed., *People for the People* (London, 1973), covers similar ground.

irrationality which loses sight of the extraordinarily articulate and disciplined nature of Chartist writing, speaking and organization. So any attempt at a total picture must always keep a balance between the unifying factors and the divisive ones, the local peculiarities and the large areas of national agreement, the overt, articulate, rational and programmatic aspects of the movement and the undefined areas of response at a different level to the pressures of industrialization, including responses by whole communities, informed by values which may have roots in older societies and traditions.

Where does Chartism begin? It is obviously inadequate to begin with the publication of the People's Charter in May 1838. Work on the unstamped press has shown the importance of this whole episode not only in providing experience of organization and a sense of a national movement, but in accentuating the hostility between the working and middle classes, and in building up the working-class consciousness, which was an essential ingredient in Chartism.[2] The whole question of the popular end of the Reform Bill agitation of 1831–1832 is of great importance in this discussion. The provincial leadership of early Chartism was to a very large extent recruited from men whose reputations as 'town radicals' was based on the manhood suffrage movement in the Reform Bill period, and who had a continuous history of agitating on radical issues in the years between. Peter Bussey, Matthew Fletcher and many other delegates to the National Convention of 1839, are examples of this.[3] They had been leaders of the

---

2. J. Weiner, *The War of the Unstamped* (London, 1969); J. Halstead, 'The Voice of the West Riding: Promoters and Supporters of a Provincial Unstamped Newspaper, 1833–34', in C. Wrigley and J. Shepherd, eds, *On the Move: Essays in Labour and Transport History* (1991), pp. 22–57.

3. Peter Bussey (1805–69) was a Bradford publican. He was in a delegation that presented a petition to Lord Melbourne calling for a pardon for the Tolpuddle labourers in 1834. Fearing arrest after his involvement in underground insurrectionary planning in winter 1839–40, he escaped to America, where he remained for fourteen years. Matthew Fletcher (1795–1878) was a Bury surgeon and steadfast campaigner for factory reform; he was active in Chartism in 1838–39. For local leaders, there is much to be

protest against the sentences of the Tolpuddle labourers in 1834 and of the Glasgow cotton spinners in 1838, had collected money and signatures in support of these protests, and in support of the Canadian rebels in 1837, had led demonstrations against the New Poor Law and the proposals for rural police and in favour of the ten hours campaign and the repeal of the Corn Laws (before the Anti-Corn Law League appropriated the campaign), and had led other campaigns on matters ranging from game laws to press freedom. The picture, originating with Francis Place, of the London artisans thinking up a political programme and then sending it out into the backward provinces, where it became converted to the visceral radicalism of inarticulate protest, simply does not bear examination.

An astonishing aspect of Chartism is the extent to which a common language was forged in an age when demotic speech and dialect must have been potentially a divisive factor. Thus Lloyd Jones, an Owenite missionary, could find R. J. Richardson 'almost uncouth by his rude provincialism of speech and awkwardness of manner' when he debated with the Anti-Corn League lecturer James Acland at Salford. But Richardson, as we know from his published writings, was a highly articulate and well-educated man. Little if any hint of provincial mannerisms appears in his writing. But to a Lancashire audience his local accent obviously paid off, since he appears to have won the debate with acclaim.[4] Much of the most effective activity, from mass meetings to exclusive dealing and the picketing of shops, could only be carried on in a sympathetic, or at worst a neutral, atmosphere. The almost total lack of information available to the authorities in many areas suggests a

---

learned from C. Godfrey, *Chartist Lives: The Anatomy of a Working-Class Movement* (London, 1987).

4. Reginald John Richardson (1808–61), a newsagent, was a very important – though seemingly peevish – Lancashire Chartist, involved 'in every movement that has taken place amongst the working classes that I can remember'. He undertook lecturing tours, and produced tracts, notably *The Rights of Women* (London, 1840). See P. A. Pickering, *Chartism and the Chartists in Manchester and Salford* (London, 1995), pp. 202–4.

considerable degree of community participation, and other evidence supports this – the driving from Ashton of two shopkeepers by an effective boycott who gave evidence against Joseph Raynor Stephens, the success of pro-Chartist shopkeepers and publicans in other areas, the events at Llanidloes and the escape of many of the Newport Chartists.[5] Connected with this is the question of police or other control in the communities. A very inadequate glance at the evidence presented in support of the demand for more effective policing in the provinces suggests that there may be a correlation between areas which had a reputation for lawlessness and areas with a high level of Chartist activity. Incidentally, some of the conservative rhetoric to be found in Chartism, which has misled some writers into seeing the movement as backward-looking or even as deferential, is connected to the opposition to the proposals for centralized police and to the New Poor Law. Some of the rhetoric is ironic, some genuinely opposed to the innovations proposed by the Reformed Parliament, which many Chartists believed were part of an all-out attack on trade union and other democratic organizations, but seldom if ever was it in support of conservative policies put forward by either of the two major parties.

How violent a movement was Chartism? And when did the change occur in the temper of the movement, from one of the constant expectation of violent provocation by the authorities to one in which the prospect of the violent overthrow of existing authority became the province only of the consciously insurrectionary wing? My own view is that this 'de-fusing' of Chartism occurred when the sentences on

---

5. For J. R. Stephens see M. Edwards, *Purge this Realm* (London, 1994). Stephens was charged with making a seditious speech at an unlawful meeting at Hyde; he was imprisoned for eighteen months. For examples of pro-Chartist shopkeepers see advertisements from John Manning (tea merchant) and George Streetley (proprietor of a hat shop) in *Midland Counties Illuminator*, 10 April 1841. The arrival of policemen in Llanidloes in April 1839 to arrest local Chartists provoked a violent community response: see O. R. Ashton, 'Chartism in Llanidloes: the "Riot" of 1839 Revisited', in *Llafur* X (2010), 76–86.

John Frost, Zephaniah Williams and William Jones were commuted to transportation in January 1840. This act by the government (against the wishes of the great majority of the cabinet) raised doubts about the fundamental violence of the authorities, and also appeared to be the result of peaceful constitutional pressure. Combined with the overwhelming defeat of the Newport Chartists, it provided an atmosphere in which the old-style radicals, the Jacobin-type leadership represented by Frost himself and by men like Bussey and Fletcher, withdrew, leaving younger men in the leading positions, men on the whole determinedly working-class in their allegiances, who reorganized the movement, and developed a variety of forms of activity and organization.

But insurrection was not the only form of violence in the society of the time. Let us take the example of Huddersfield. In 1831 20,000 people assembled to burn a bishop in effigy; in 1837 tens of thousands in the same area attacked the Poor Law Commissioners and prevented the implementation of the 1834 Act for over a year and effectively moderated its eventual application; in 1839 there was drilling on the surrounding hills but no outbreak; in 1842 there was massive support for the strikers but no actual clash with the military or special constables; in 1848 again there was drilling and a number of arrests, but no clashes. The interesting thing was that Chartism appears here to have reduced the violence in the community – the folk-violence of effigy-burning and the direct action of the anti-Poor Law campaign gave way to the disciplined organization of the Chartists in which thousands could gather, often with arms, often in conditions of great political tension or economic distress, and yet remain completely peaceful.[6]

What of the relationship between Chartism and later movements? The view that the Liberal Party was getting more and more democratic, and that if the Chartists had

---

6. See J. A. Hargreaves, 'A Metropolis of Discontent: Popular Protest in Huddersfield c. 1780–c. 1850', in E. A. H. Haigh, ed., *Huddersfield: A Most Handsome Town* (Kirklees, 1992), pp. 189–220.

only waited until 1867 they would have got an important part of their programme has been challenged, and it is now recognized that the movement towards the democratization of the Liberal Party was affected not only by the experience of Chartism, but by the actual participation in local politics of Chartists and ex-Chartists. But this apparent coming together of the two movements has in fact been one of the difficulties in studying Chartism in the past. In the high noon of Gladstonian Liberalism, Chartism received a certain aura of respectability, and the memoirs of former Chartists were welcomed by Liberal newspapers as offering a contrast between the bad old days of the Corn Laws and the blessings of free trade. The illiberal Chartism of drilling and arming, or of communitarian experiment, was suppressed in favour of this premature Gladstonian image, and the few disgruntled or romantic characters – Matthew Fletcher, Thomas Ainge Devyr and Alexander Somerville – were dismissed as sensationalists. But all the reminiscences are unreliable in their different ways, and all must be checked against contemporary sources. And by these tests some of the more sensational accounts, which have been dismissed, still seem to me to have important elements of truth in them.[7]

---

7. Thomas Ainge Devyr (1805–77) was an Irish-born journalist who was involved in the insurrectionary wing of Chartism in 1838–40, leading to his hasty departure for America where he edited more journals and brought out his memoir, *The Odd Book of the Nineteenth Century* (New York, 1882). Alexander Somerville, the author of *Dissuasive Warnings to the People on Street Warfare* (London, 1839) and *The Autobiography of a Working Man* (London, 1848), was hostile to Chartism.

2

THE LANGUAGES OF CLASS

Gareth Stedman Jones is a writer whose work has stimulated a good deal of discussion among labour and other historians.[1] His essay 'Rethinking Chartism' has received much attention, enthusiastic and critical, and is worth looking at in detail. The first point to be made is that this essay is not in fact primarily concerned with language; not, that is, if one accepts a definition of language which includes forms of communication going beyond the printed word. Language must surely go beyond the examination of political concepts as expressed in the leading articles of journals to include other means of expression and other forms of communication, verbal and non-verbal.

Stedman Jones reminds us that Chartism was a political movement. His argument here is cogent, and a valuable corrective to the 'trade cycle' view of events. But historians of Chartism have been disconcerted by some of the conclusions he has arrived at by returning to a political analysis. He is also, incidentally, rather less than just to some contemporary and subsequent

---

1. This essay was originally published in *Bulletin of the Society for the Study of Labour History* 52:1 (1987), 54–7. The opening paragraphs have been abbreviated.

historians and commentators. Although it is true that, following Thomas Carlyle, many contemporaries accepted a purely social interpretation of the movement, others, including Benjamin Disraeli, were very much aware of its political dimension. Carlyle's famous definition is more often quoted, but it should be remembered that Disraeli's Two Nations were divided not only by different food and different manners, but were not governed by the same laws.[2] Disraeli's Chartists were certainly politicians, women as well as men.

What concerns and has provoked those familiar with the basic material from which the history of Chartism has been written is the implication that Chartism was somehow not a working-class movement. Since participants and observers at the time clearly regarded it as such, an analysis which treats their views as misapprehensions raises a number of questions. Setting aside for the moment methodological doubts about the validity of a fundamental revision based on the partial examination of one type of evidence only, the questions involved seem to me to be of two orders. One sort of comment has been to suggest that Stedman Jones has made basic misjudgements about the very question with which he has concerned himself, that his definition of language is unacceptable to modern scholarship, and that his reading, even of printed material, is inadequate and selective to an impermissible degree. The other major concern is that behind the discussion lurks a definition of 'class' which is never clearly stated, but against which Chartist responses are measured and found wanting. An assumed Marxist definition may be based on the acceptance of a view which has shown itself to be inadequate to describe or analyse the social structures of many non-European cultures – has indeed been responsible for serious political and social misreadings in countries such as India and China. If fundamentals are up for discussion, perhaps the adequacy of the class definition lurking in the wings of the essay should be examined first.

---

2. In *Chartism* (London, 1839), Carlyle famously described Chartism as 'bitter discontent grown fierce and mad'.

But if we are, nevertheless, to look at the kind of language being considered, it is immediately clear that there is a serious lack of context in the presentation of the quotations. There is a scene in the *Pirates of Penzance* in which the hero, Frederic, having as he thought finished his apprenticeship to the pirates, is shown that he had in fact been sworn until his twenty-first birthday and, since he had been born in leap year on 29 February, had another seventy-odd years to serve. His former associates remind him of his duty and the sacredness of his oath, and he reluctantly agrees to return. Listeners to a broadcast of the opera would assume that Frederic was behaving like the 'slave of duty' that the plot was sending up. In the theatre, of course, it is clear that the rational argument and appeal to high motives are backed up by loaded pistols held to either ear. The Chartist appeal to the middle class had the loaded pistols of huge crowds, torchlight meetings, millions of signatures and arming and drilling in communities in which the control of police and magistrates was minimal. What is more, by the time of the publication of the People's Charter, a wholly Protestant Parliament had given in to the combination of rational argument and the presence outside of millions of committed Irish Catholics intent on seeing their candidates elected, and had granted Catholic emancipation. A Parliament based on a franchise heavily over-representing the landed interest had given in to a similar combination of arguments for natural justice and a country demonstrating and rioting for reform, and admitted new forms of wealth to the franchise. It may be argued that in neither case was the capitulation as straightforward as it seemed, but at the time, to the Chartists, there seemed strong precedents for precisely this kind of tactic.

As T. A. Devyr made clear in his widely distributed *Appeal to the Middle Classes* (1839), the Chartists would clearly have preferred the reasonable members of the other classes, particularly the working sections of the middle class who shared some of their disabilities, to support them and help to pressurize Parliament to widen the franchise. The few members of Parliament who did support them in this and in their other demands were indeed admired and praised (why not?). But behind the arguments from natural rights and natural justice lay the mass meeting and the threat of armed rising. Devyr specifically says, and was arrested for saying so, that the alternative for the middle class, if the Charter was not achieved peacefully with their help, was the destruction of their families and the firing of their shops and factories: 'Your warehouses and your homes will be given to the flames, and one black ruin overwhelm England.' The appeal for manhood suffrage and an open, constantly-renewed Parliament elected by citizens whose votes were protected by the ballot and made of equal value by a redistribution of seats may have been similar to the programmes of the London Corresponding Society and of Major John Cartwright. But the context in which it was proposed was very different. In still another context it was exactly the same programme which was put forward in 1791 by the United Irishmen and which led them directly into participation in the biggest rising against the British Government since the seventeenth century. This, too, was part of the context in which the Chartists put forward their arguments.

But as well as the significance of context, there is a lot more to be said about the actual rhetoric, vocabulary and semiotics of the movement than is admitted into Stedman Jones's argument. When the Chartists, for instance, at suppers or at fund-raising performances toasted the memory of the Irish republican Robert Emmett or recited his speech from the dock, they were signalling admiration for someone who had been publicly hanged and decapitated for treason in the memory of most living people. The Cap of Liberty and the Tricolour signalled support for the early days of the French Revolution, and were to be seen regularly at Chartist rallies. When Feargus O'Connor, dressed in a suit of fustian, submitted his name for election to the executive of the National Charter Association, he was making gestures towards egalitarianism and democratic control which went far beyond anything in the political vocabulary of Henry Hunt or William Cobbett.

In contrast even middle-class political reformers like Thomas Babbington Macaulay and Charles Kingsley viewed manhood suffrage with abhorrence. The small number of established politicians who made a short-lived attempt to detach an acceptable group of working men from Chartism to mount a joint campaign for suffrage extension were as unpopular with members of their own class as they were with the mainstream Chartists. As one middle-class sympathizer later expressed it, the Chartists brought 'discredit to their principles by a rash, theatrical and violent method of asserting them'. The confrontation was in the manner as well as the content of Chartist demands.

There is no space here to urge the importance to the consideration of the language of Chartism of the material to be found in reports of speeches which did not appear in print. Spies' reports, trial documents, magistrates' letters and other sources often reveal a sharper and more aggressive rhetoric. Statements have to be examined in context. Chartists in the dock were often defending themselves against the heaviest sentences, and their statements in such a context cannot be given the same weight as newspaper editorials. But these too represent a particular public tone. Radical papers were operating on the fringes of legality and were for many reasons obliged to adopt a tone of rationality and even-handed argument which will not be found in reports of semi-legal and private meetings. All are part of the language.

But, it may be argued, even if the argument was presented in a more forceful and confrontational manner, it was still the argument of class collaboration, since a truly working-class programme for the time would have consisted of the demand for the expropriation of the expropriators and would have stressed economic change rather than political. It is at this point that the idea of 'false consciousness' has to be considered. It is tempting to assume that historians, with the advantages of hindsight and of access to information not available to contemporaries, can say what the appropriate programme for each class should have been at a particular time, and can then judge the true class nature of movements by the degree to which they approached their true consciousness. It is a Leninist, perhaps a Platonic, idea which has great attractions. Other labour historians have indeed assumed that a working-class movement should have a socialist consciousness, and that, by limiting their demands to political aims, Chartists dug their own grave. Stedman Jones makes essentially this argument, suggesting that since political demands rested on fear of politically repressive action by the state, when this fear was allayed by the liberalization of the state, the movement for reform died.

In this form the argument is over-simplified. It is no new discovery to suggest that the decline of Chartism is to be explained by the loss of confidence in political action by the excluded classes who had mounted the demonstrations and signed the petitions. The study of Chartism is the study of a political phase of working-class experience. Its decline occurred as faith in politics and a concomitant fear of political monopoly faded. One aspect of this decline of fear *may* have been the liberalization of the state, though I have doubts about this, and it is here asserted rather than demonstrated. Perhaps more relevant was the toning down of the activities of the enthusiastic Whig reformers after 1837, for it was the series of developments in the immediately post-reform years, from the Irish Coercion Act of 1833 to the 'finality' speech of Lord John Russell in 1837, and including the two legal cases of the Tolpuddle labourers and the Glasgow cotton spinners, that turned all working-class activity towards political action. After that the philosophic radicals declined as a political force, and Whig and Tory administrations alike held back on centralizing measures. Even the unpopular provisions of the 1839 Rural Police Act were introduced far more cautiously that those of the 1834 Poor Law Amendment Act, with permissive regulations allowing local initiatives, but with no compulsion for nearly another two decades. The New Poor Law itself relapsed into greater localism and reverted to more traditional practices after 1847. In spite of the high level of coercive action

by the state in 1848, it may well have appeared less threatening, and control of the legislative processes have
appeared less essential for the escape from working-class
dilemmas.

It is probably more true to suggest that the experience of
the radical and Chartist decades modified some attitudes in
all sections of those holding power. Larger employers
changed their tone and provided some space for the emergence of new-style trade unions among skilled workmen.
Co-operative Societies, Friendly Societies and Regeneration
and other societies took off as the result of rather more
regular and stable earnings in the manufacturing districts.
The repeal of the Corn Laws and the passing of the Ten
Hours Act made even clearer the lesson that many radicals
had already drawn from the reprieve of the Newport leaders – that even a corrupt Parliament could respond to
external pressure. But perhaps the most important influences in the field of ideas were the teachings of political
economy and of nascent socialism both of which denied the
power of political action, a lesson which was to be reinforced by events in France between 1848 and 1852. The
panacea of manhood suffrage ceased to wield its magic –
and England was indeed to be one of the last industrialized
countries to achieve it.

None of this, however, alters the fact that, if the
concept of class means anything, Chartism was a working-class movement. Its language at all levels was class
language: the concepts of manhood suffrage, the rights of
man and of equality of citizenship were only held by the
lower orders, the working class or classes. The sense of
class solidarity for a time overrode regional, occupa-
tional, ethnic and gender divisions in ways that were not
to recur for generations. The demand for control over
their work, for access to landholdings, the desire for the
independence of a smallholding or workshop may seem
to some Marxists to be inappropriate to the aspirations
of a working class. But it should be noted that these aspirations were strongest among the most industrialized
workers – that the Land Plan, for example, had its most

enthusiastic support among the cotton factory workers of Ashton-under-Lyne.[3]

To persuade the middle class to support their arguments for political rights the Chartists used two tactics, that of rational persuasion and that of threats and loaded weapons of various kinds. By considering only one of these, Gareth Stedman Jones underestimates the threat posed by Chartism to the established order and the class nature of the movement. This essay illustrates one of the dangers of bringing too many theoretical preconceptions to the study of historical evidence. A close study of the history of the working people and working-class movements – of which Chartism is among the most important in British history – will inevitably lead us to modify and elaborate our definitions. It is to be hoped that this essay will continue to provoke discussion around this subject.[4]

3.   For Ashton-under-Lyne see R. G. Hall, *Voices of the People* (London, 2007).

4.   See J. Foster, 'The Declassing of Language', *New Left Review* 150 (1985), 29–45; J. Epstein, 'The Working Class and the People's Charter', *International Labor and Working Class History* 28 (Fall 1985), 69–78; P. Mandler, 'Left Social History – British Versions', *Dissent* (Summer 1985), 351–3; P. A. Pickering, 'Class Without Words: Symbolic Communication in the Chartist Movement', *Past and Present* 112 (August 1986), 144–62; J. Epstein, *Radical Expression: Political Language, Ritual and Symbol in England, 1790–1850* (Oxford, 1995); M. Taylor, 'Rethinking the Chartists: Searching for Synthesis in the Historiography of Chartism', *Historical Journal* 39:2 (1996), 479–95; A. Messner, 'Land, Leadership, Culture and Emigration: Some Problems in Chartist Historiography', *Historical Journal* 42:2 (1999), 1093–1109; M. Roberts, *Political Movements in Urban England 1832–1914* (2009); J. Allen and M. Chase, 'Britain: 1750–1900', in J. Allen, A. Campbell and J. McIlroy, eds, *Worlds of Labour* (London, 2011), pp. 70–5.

3

WHO WERE 'THE PEOPLE' IN 1842?

In his history of the common people, J. F. C. Harrison recalls the story of little Joseph Arch, at the age of seven, peeping through the keyhole of the parish church to watch the adults receiving holy communion.[1] The sight of the separation of the congregation by class, with the labourers going humbly to the altar rail after their social betters had received the host, gave him a sudden and immediate awareness of the divisions in his society and 'the iron entered into my poor little heart and remained fast embedded there'.[2] By 1842, the year I want to look at in this essay, the teenage Arch was risking his job as well as the charitable gifts of food, blankets and coal on which labouring families relied in times of bad weather or ill-health, to attend the dissenting services held in semi-secrecy in the open air or in the shelter of farm buildings. His quarrel was not with the tenets of Christianity nor, at least initially, with the terms in which it was presented by the Anglican Church; it was certainly not with the language of the Bible or the Book of Common Prayer. He was alienated by the context in which

---

1. This essay was originally published in M. Chase and I. Dyck, eds, *Living and Learning* (Aldershot, 1996), pp. 118–32.
2. J. F. C. Harrison, *The Common People* (London, 1984), p. 282.

these things were offered to the villagers. The language of religion, as, in other situations, that of politics, has to be seen in precise context if it is to illuminate the actions of the people employing it.

In this essay, I want to raise some of the questions which have to be asked about the use of language as a major historical 'source'. To what extent does the language of politics have a fixed set of meanings, irrespective of who is speaking and under what constraints, who is being addressed, who is reporting the speech, and what forms of communication other than verbal are involved such as dress, accent and gender? Put in this simple form the question appears absurd. Everyone is aware, for example, that an order in a public house in a mining district in the nineteenth century for a pint of beer and a whisky chaser would not raise an eyebrow if it was given by a miner, but the same order in the identical words given by an unaccompanied young lady would cause uproar. An order for tea and scones in a posh London hotel would see the roles reversed, if indeed the unconventional customer in either case could manage to gain admission to the premises: signals given by dress, bearing and gender would have decided the question of their treatment before a word had been spoken. The words alone tell us little about the social issues involved.

Much of the discussion about political rhetoric does, at base, lack the essential element of context. The idea of a democratic anti-court rhetoric originating with the 'country party', picked up by John Wilkes and John Cartwright in the eighteenth century, dominating the political language of post-Napoleonic War political radicalism into Chartism and beyond carries with it the idea that the programmes of the various political or social movements which employed versions of this rhetoric were basically the same, and that a programme has the same meaning in the mouths of a small aristocratic clique as on the banners of a procession of 10,000 armed coal and iron workers in South Wales. But at any particular moment in history, the meaning given to words and phrases is influenced by precisely the factors which too many of the 'language' school of interpreters set aside: the class, the interest and the power relations of those who employ them.

It is a truism that words, slogans and concepts have very different force at different times in history. As Marc Bloch remarked many years ago: 'To the great despair of historians, men fail to change their vocabulary every time they change their customs.'[3] In the arena of politics, words and concepts are continually being contested. The concept of 'the people' was widely used by politicians of all shades during the nineteenth century. There may have been moments towards the end of the century when it assumed an overarching, classless, national meaning, in line perhaps with its use in the USA. In Britain, however, in the 1840s, it can only be understood in the context of a class-divided society. To read it as a neutral, classless term would be to misread the politics, parliamentary and popular, of the period.

In her speech from the throne at the opening of Parliament in February 1842, Victoria spoke of 'the continued distress in the manufacturing districts of the country' and of 'the sufferings and privations which have resulted from it'. She expressed her confidence that the deliberations of Parliament and the measures which they proposed would be 'directed by a comprehensive regard for the interests and permanent welfare of all classes of my subjects, and I fervently pray that they may tend in their results to improve the national resources and to encourage the industry and promote the happiness of my people'.[4] It is hard from this not to conclude that the people in the last phrase are the lower classes of her subjects whose industry needs promoting rather more than that of the higher orders. For virtually all of those who spoke in the parliamentary debates in the course of that year, the expression 'the people' was unequivocally reserved for the lower orders. Thus, Sir Robert Peel, Prime Minister in the new Tory administration, praised 'the forbearance of the people' in these distressing times, but deprecated 'motions making the government

---

3. M. Bloch, *The Historian's Craft* (Manchester, 1954), p. 57.
4. Hansard, LXI, 3 February 1842.

responsible for providing them with sustenance and employment'.[5] Among the more radical Whigs, Charles Pelham Villiers pointed out that 'the people, being neither Whig nor Tory, were disposed to think that the monopolies springing out of what they termed class legislation had so far exhausted their means and restricted their energies as to be answerable for the decline of this great industrial nation.'[6] Charles Brotherton, a manufacturer, believed that 'the people were beginning to understand the causes of their distress' which he saw as poverty and lack of sufficient food; he declared that his own principle would always be 'perish party but give the people bread'.[7]

The term 'the people' to mean the excluded, the unenfranchised, was widely employed. Ebenezer Elliott's 'People's Anthem' embodies it:

> When wilt thou save the people?
> O God of mercy! When?
> Not kings and lords but nations!
> Not thrones and crowns but men!
> Flowers of thy heart, O God, are they?
> Let them not pass like weeds away!
> Their heritage a sunless day!
> God save the people!

In 1861, when he had been converted to a limited extension of the franchise, Lord John Russell defined 'the people' as 'the working classes'.[8] If this usage was challenged, it was among old-fashioned, country Tories, not among the political spokesmen of any parliamentary group. James Vernon cites a speaker, at a Devonshire Conservative banquet in

5.   1 July 1842, reported in J. Irving, *The Annals of Our Time from June 20 1837 to February 28 1871* (London, 1890), p. 112.

6.   A Member of the Cobden Club, ed., *The Free Trade Speeches of the Rt. Hon. Charles Pelham Villiers* (London, 1883), p. 322. Villiers took the lead in the House of Commons in calling for the repeal of the Corn Laws.

7.   Hansard, LX, 17 September 1841.

8.   Quoted in J. Parry, *The Rise and Fall of Liberal Government in Victorian Britain* (Yale, 1993), p. 209.

1837, as demanding: 'What did the radicals mean by talking about the people? . . . In the list which these liberal philosophers have drawn up, who do they call the people? They exclude the lords, the clergy, the landowners, the merchants and even their old companions the Whigs.'[9] In the political debates of 1842 no one challenged the usage which excluded those categories.

The National Petition of 1842 consisted of the six points of the People's Charter with around forty accompanying paragraphs. A petition calling for reforms in line with the six points – for an extension of the suffrage, shorter parliaments and vote by secret ballot – had been introduced earlier in the year. It had received little support but little hostility either. The Chartist petition was received very differently by speakers from both major parties. The Chartists were not allowed to speak to their own petition. The proposal that a delegation representing the signatories be received at the Bar of the House of Commons was put, debated and thoroughly defeated. The case for hearing the Chartists was put by a small group whom Richard Oastler called the 'philanthropic' radicals, as opposed to the 'philosophic' or free trade variety.[10] On nearly all the subjects that divided the Chartists from the Anti-Corn Law League, these took the Chartist side. Thomas Slingsby Duncombe, the radical old Etonian nephew of Lord Feversham, was by 1842 sitting for the radical London borough of Finsbury. Friedrich Engels described him as 'the representative of the working men in the House of Commons' and he certainly spoke up consistently on behalf of the Chartists, as well as presenting forcefully the case for admission of their representatives to speak to their petition.[11] Thomas Wakley, Duncombe's fellow member for Finsbury, had referred to himself, in proposing an amendment in favour of the secret

---

9. Quoted in J. Vernon, *Politics and the People* (Cambridge, 1993), p. 314.

10. *Fleet Papers*, 12 March 1842 and passim.

11. F. Engels, *The Condition of the Working Class in England* (London, 1892 edn.), p. 17. For Duncombe, see S. Roberts in *The House of Commons 1832–1868* (forthcoming).

ballot to the Queen's Speech in 1837, as 'a representative of labour'.[12] A radical who refused to use any of the normal electoral devices, even including canvassing, Wakley was a surgeon by profession and editor of the campaigning *Lancet*. He spoke with a strong provincial accent – that of his native Dorset – and was not above entertaining the House with anecdotes in the vernacular.[13] John Fielden, whose provincial accent was held to be so strong as to make his contributions in the House all but incomprehensible to southerners, was the head of the largest cotton manufacturer in Europe; he had declared in his initial election address in 1833 that 'nothing but an anxious solicitude to see the people restored to their just rights, and especially the labouring population of society greatly improved, could have induced him to enter Parliament'.[14] These three were the main supporters of the Chartist petition in the House, and were joined in the division lobby by fewer than fifty assorted radicals and eccentrics.

None of these parliamentary spokesmen could be held to have been using the actual words of the working people who had drawn up and signed the petition. These appeared only in the text, nearly every paragraph of which refers to 'the people'.[15] The petition announced itself as 'The petition of the undersigned people of the United Kingdom', and proceeded to show 'That the Government originated from and was designed to protect the freedom and promote the happiness of, and ought to be responsible to, the whole

12. C. Brook, *Thomas Wakley* (London, 1942), p. 24; J. Hostettler, *Thomas Wakley* (Chichester, 1993).

13. One of No Party, *Random Recollections of the House of Commons* (London, 1836), pp. 252–4.

14. J. Holden, *A Short History of Todmorden* (Manchester, 1912), pp. 163–4.

15. *The National Petition of the Industrious Classes* (Leeds, 1842). The petition is printed in *Hansard*, LXV. All the quotations below are from the petition and are not separately footnoted. For a time the fragment held at the Working Class Movement Library was thought to be part of the 1842 Chartist petition; but it now seems more likely to have been one of the numerous petitions noted in *Hansard* (eg., 20 March 1840, 3 May 1841) that were presented in favour of, or in opposition to, the repeal of the Corn Laws.

people'. In almost every one of the itemized grievances 'the people' are taken to be the unenfranchised, alternating with expressions such as 'working men' or specific groups such as agricultural labourers where particular hardships are being emphasized. Only in the Irish section can the term perhaps be read as having a wider significance: 'That your petitioners complain of the many grievances borne by the people of Ireland; and contend that they are fully entitled to a repeal of the Legislative Union.' Even here, though, it could be argued that it was the unenfranchised Irish, not the property owners there, whose interests were being pressed. The term otherwise is used unambiguously:

> That the only authority on which any body of men can make laws and govern society is delegation from the people ... That your Honourable House, as at present constituted, has not been elected by, and acts irresponsibly, of the people ... Your Honourable House has enacted laws contrary to the expressed wishes of the people and hitherto has only represented parties and represented the few, regardless of the miseries, grievances and petitions of the many.

Macaulay's comment that manhood suffrage 'would be fatal to all purposes for which government exists and for which aristocracies and all other things exist and ... is utterly incompatible with the very existence of civilization' is well known.[16] Peel's response was hardly less comprehensive:

> The petition tells me that it is wrong to maintain an established church – it says that £9 million of money are annually abstracted from the people for the purpose of maintaining the church. The petition tells me that the people of Ireland are entitled to a repeal of the union. The petition draws a most invidious comparison between the expenses of the sovereign and those of a labourer. I say the petition is

---

16.   Hansard, LXIII, 3 May 1842.

altogether an impeachment of the constitution of this country and of the whole frame of society.[17]

Russell, the presenter of the 1832 Reform Act and the
proponent of the 'finality' of its provisions, added his voice
to the condemnation of the petition:

> In the present state of popular education – I will not say
> whether a standard of education sufficiently high can ever
> be obtained among the labouring classes – but in the pres-
> ent condition of the people at large, I do not think you can
> be sure that there might not be, in the state of popular
> ferment on the occasion of some general election, Members
> returned to this House whose votes would be favourable to
> the destruction of our institutions and would shake the
> security of property.[18]

These reactions suggest that it was the context, particularly
the extra-parliamentary context of the petition, which
produced the response rather than the wording or the
specific objects for which it called.

Within Parliament, then, 'the people' were clearly seen
as the lower orders, the labouring population, whose
demand for the vote was associated with at best disre-
spect for authority and at worst with the intention to
overthrow the whole edifice of parliamentary government. Outside, too, the authorities in general seem to
have used it in the same way. Thus, Lord Justice Denman,
addressing 150 Chartists in the dock, in September 1842,
complained:

> Unfortunately it was a matter for astonishment and lamen-
> tation that, after all that had been done to enlighten and
> educate the people – and he would fearlessly add – to
> improve their condition and improve their comforts – there
> should still be found in this country men, by the hundred

---

17. Ibid.
18. Ibid.

and thousand, ready to assemble together for the absurd, the insane, the suicidal purpose of throwing men in their own circumstances out of employment and thus increasing terribly the distress which unhappily existed.[19]

The return of the Tories to power in 1841 had released some of the more radical elements among the Liberals from their support for the Whig government. The Anti-Corn Law League was not above appealing for the support of working men, and even contemplated what Villiers referred to as 'the brickbat argument' to drive home their belief in the connection between protection and the depression.[20] Much of their language sounded as subversive as that of the Chartists, while some of their tactics went even further in appearing to define the legal limits of political activity. But their campaigning in 1842 failed signally either to win over any substantial section of the radical working men or to establish a common 'populist' rhetoric which could have transcended class barriers.

The story of the relations between the Chartists and the Anti-Corn Law League has been told.[21] Historians of different approaches have agreed in seeing the gulf between the two movements and their failure to unite to pressurize the Tory government as being a matter of class relations in the manufacturing districts rather than a clash of ideas. The Chartist petition itself took into account the long-standing radical support for the repeal of taxes on food, but put it into broader perspective:

Your petitioners deeply deplore the existence of any kind of monopoly in this nation; and, whilst they unequivocally condemn the levying of any tax upon the necessaries of life, and upon those articles principally required by the

---

19. Irving, *Annals of Our Time*, 5 September 1842, p. 119.
20. L. Brown, 'The Chartists and the Anti-Corn Law League', in Briggs, *Chartist Studies*, p. 364.
21. N. McCord, *The Anti-Corn Law League* (London, 1958); P. A. Pickering and A. Tyrell, *The People's Bread: A History of the Anti-Corn Law League* (London, 2000).

labouring classes, they are also sensible that the abolition of any one monopoly will never unshackle labour from its misery until the people possess that power under which all monopoly and oppression must cease; and your petitioners respectfully mention the existing monopolies of the suffrage, of paper money, of machinery, of land, of the public press, of religious privileges, of the means of travelling and transit and a host of other evils too numerous to mention, all arising from class legislation, but which your Honourable House has always consistently endeavoured to increase instead of diminish.[22]

On the side of the League there was little in the way of a shared social identity, although there were a number of attempts to convince working men of a unity of interest between the classes on the issue of Corn Law repeal. A letter sent to all MPs in June 1842 declared that 'the great bulk of the people, the customers of each other and of all the other classes, are becoming too poor to purchase and thus they cease to consume.'[23] Here, clearly, the people are the lower orders, not the whole of the non-aristocratic population. It is in fact in the material put out by the League that the most consistent rhetoric of class is to be found. There were occasions on which they pleaded a common interest between the middle and working class, and others on which they offered leadership to the lower orders. I can find none in which they elided the two into a single populist category. What is more, although the tactics of the League in the early part of the year were disruptive of parliamentary conventions – as when they set up an alternative gathering as a kind of anti-parliament or marched, 500 strong, on the House of Commons and attempted to invade the lobbies – such behaviour produced nothing of the alarm and heavy condemnation which greeted the Chartist petition. Duncombe complained when the Home Secretary

---

22. *The National Petition of the Industrious Classes* (Leeds, 1842).
23. H. J. Leech, ed., *The Public Letters of the Rt. Hon. John Bright* (London, 1885), p. 332.

defended the arrest and imprisonment of a group of Birmingham Chartists:

> If the language used by Mason at that meeting was seditious and was sufficient to justify the constables to interfere and disperse the assembly, why did not the police break up and disperse other bodies of men, at whose meetings language infinitely stronger than any that Mason used was daily heard? Why not break in and disperse the meetings of the delegates of the Anti-Corn Law League which were held daily within a stone's throw of the House of Commons?[24]

Although some of the rhetoric used annoyed local magistrates, on the whole Anti-Corn Law League speakers were allowed much greater latitude than the Chartists, hundreds of whom served sentences for speeches made in 1842. Not a single member of the League was charged, although, if rhetoric alone is being discussed, it has to be admitted that that employed by the Leaguers often ran the Chartists pretty close. It would indeed be difficult to find Chartists competing with the speech given by the Leeds Liberal J. C. Nussey in October 1841, in which he 'begged to remind Queen Victoria that the heads of better sovereigns had rolled in the dust and declared that, unless the condition of the people were bettered, the flag of revolution would be hoisted and the streets swim in blood'.[25] Young Mr Nussey's speech appears to have been listened to, and reported on in the local press, without any apparent concern on the part of the authorities.

Whigs, Tories and Leaguers responded to the spoken and written word according not only to the content but to the class of the speaker. They used the concept of class

---

24. Hansard, LXV, 4 August 1842. John Mason arrived in Birmingham as an NCA lecturer. He was a very talented orator, delivering a powerful speech before a huge crowd on the Wrekin in April 1842. Mason rejected O'Connor's leadership in favour of Bronterre O'Brien, but was still arrested in July 1842 after addressing a meeting of Black Country strikers.

25. Quoted in G. Kitson Clark, 'Hunger and Politics in 1842', *Journal of Modern History* 25 (1953), 355–74.

continually. John Bright, alarmed by the strikes and demonstrations in his native Rochdale, wrote an open letter to local working men. In it he told them that any attempt to increase wages or to shorten hours was to go against the laws of nature. On the suffrage there was more room for manoeuvre:

> Against the obtaining of the Charter, the laws of nature offer no impediment, as they do against a forcible advance of wages; but to obtain the Charter now is just as impossible as to raise wages by force. The aristocracy are powerful and determined; and, unhappily, the middle classes are not yet intelligent enough to see the safety of extending political power to the whole people. The aristocracy regard the Anti-Corn Law League as their greatest enemy. That which is the greatest enemy of the remorseless aristocracy of Britain must also of necessity be your firmest friend.[26]

Richard Cobden, in some ways more sympathetic in his language at this time to the hardships of the working population, hoped that 'the capitalists of Lancashire were sufficiently enlightened as to their own interests to know that the worst thing for them would be to have a badly remunerated working population'.[27] When it came to organized workers, however, Cobden did no better than Bright. In a letter to the League President George Wilson, in late 1841, he spoke of having tried to get some action going in Birmingham, where the Complete Suffrage Union was strong and joint action between the middle and working classes on the Corn Law question seemed possible. But he was pessimistic: 'I called along with Jos. Sturge upon Collins and two other leaders of the new move but they are not a whit more reasonable upon our question than the O'Connorites . . . Our only plan is to leave the two Chartist factions to fight with each other & raise up a working-class

---

26. Leech, *Public Letters*, p. 336.
27. Hansard, LXV, 17 September 1842. This quotation has been slightly abbreviated.

party of repealers independent of both.'[28] By June 1842 Edward Watkin was writing to Cobden reporting the failure of attempts to foster collaboration between the classes by means of the CSU:

> The radicals who went with us before have now joined the Charter Association . . . and the poor, faithful, but ignorant and bigoted fellows who supported the Corn Law repeal as a better thing than Chartism have been disgusted at what their poor brains consider a piece of cowardly conciliation and now give very lukewarm support.[29]

There are many examples of attempts by the Leaguers in the immediate aftermath of the Tory victory to establish a joint opposition based on Corn Law repeal. In all cases the Chartists took the opportunity to get manhood suffrage motions passed, and the collaboration was stillborn. For example, a meeting called in the town hall in Manchester in June 1842 by local shopkeepers to consider the bad state of trade was attended by so many people – reported as between 10,000 and 12,000 – that it had to be adjourned to Stevenson Square. Here the platform was heard only after the intervention of the Chartist James Leach. A resolution was put to the meeting calling for the repeal of the Corn Laws. Leach responded with an amendment proposing the adoption of the Charter, and enquired: 'If the Corn Laws were repealed tomorrow, what power would the people have to protect themselves from class legislation any more than they had now?' After the Chartist resolution was carried with only a handful of dissentient votes, the

---

28. Quoted in McCord, *The Anti-Corn Law League*, pp. 115–16. This quotation has been slightly abbreviated. John Collins (1802–52), a toolmaker and later grocer, was closely associated with the Birmingham Political Union, both in its first phase in the early 1830s and during its revival later in the decade. Imprisoned with Lovett in 1839–40, he joined his National Association rather than the National Charter Association and entered into discussions with middle-class radicals.

29. Ibid. Edward Watkin, the son of the wealthy Absalom Watkin, was prominently involved in League affairs in Manchester; he later represented Stockport in Parliament.

meeting dispersed. The next day placards appeared in the town calling another meeting, this time by ticket only, which should consist of 'shopkeepers, traders, innkeepers, cottage owners and retail dealers exclusively' to consider the original resolution.[30] Co-operation between the two bodies foundered not on rhetoric or incompatibility of political concepts, but on the fact that in each community the Anti-Corn Law League case was put by employers, merchants and traders, whilst that of the Chartists was put by working people. As R. G. Gammage commented :

> There was – whatever may be thought of the policy – something heroic in the attitude assumed by working men on this question. It was a battle of the employer and the employed. Masters were astonished at what they deemed the audacity of their workmen, who made no scruple of standing beside them on the platform and contesting them face to face their most cherished doctrines. Terrible was the persecution they suffered for taking this liberty. Loss of employment usually followed, but it was in vain that their employers endeavoured to starve them into submission.[31]

It was not only in their confrontation with the League that working men began to enter public areas which had hitherto been the domain of the property-owning and educated classes. The early years of Chartism saw the invasion of churches; the later years saw some attempts to penetrate the vestries, nominally open to all parishioners but in fact usually the preserve of the men from the rank of shopkeeper upwards.[32] The Chartists began to assert a local

---

30. *Northern Star*, 6 August 1842. James Leach (1806–69), a factory operative and later a bookseller, was a Manchester Chartist with a national reputation. He led the attack on repeal of the Corn Laws and amongst his writings was *Stubborn Facts from the Factories* (London, 1844). See P. A. Pickering, *Chartism and the Chartists in Manchester and Salford*, pp. 198–9.

31. R. G. Gammage, *History of the Chartist Movement* (London, 1969 edn.), pp. 216–17.

32. E. Yeo, 'Christianity in Chartist Struggle', in S. Roberts, ed., *The People's Charter: Democratic Agitation in Early Victorian Britain* (London, 2003), pp. 64–93.

working-class presence, particularly on occasions on which the church rate was being discussed. The Halifax Chartist Benjamin Wilson made it clear how uncomfortable an individual workman could feel at such meetings.[33] In 1842 working men used the power of numbers to boost their confidence, as they did with their taking over of anti-Corn Law meetings. At Keighley, in July 1842, the vestry met to set the parish rate for the coming year:

> At five minutes to eleven Mr Busfield the parish parson, attended by a group of pot-bellied landlords, two magistrates, two or three brandy-spinners, two auctioneers, a deputy constable, a number of bum bailiffs, lawyers and others to the number of thirty entered the church. At eleven the vestry door opened and in rushed the working men to the number of three hundred.

The meeting was adjourned to the churchyard, but had to be abandoned without a rate having been set.[34] Like the overturning of meetings of the Anti-Corn Law League, this episode illustrates a victory of numbers over custom and protocol. The working man attempting to enter an area to which he had nominal rights found himself often at the mercy of the symbolic power of language which Pierre Bourdieu has anatomized.[35] The words used in the conduct of the institutions of local authority carry quite different weights according to who is using them. The problems experienced during the gradual entry of working men, and then of women, into these institutions illustrates the ways in which 'official language' was used as an instrument of class power. As with all the considerations of language the exact context and the status of the speaker or writer is at least as important as the actual words used.

---

33. B. Wilson, 'The Struggles of an Old Chartist', in D. Vincent, ed., *Testaments of Radicalism* (London, 1977), p. 203.
34. *Northern Star*, 30 July 1842.
35. P. Bourdieu, *Language and Symbolic Power* (London, 1992).

To a large extent, the Chartists used the term 'the people' interchangeably with 'the working class'. Thus, George White, writing to Thomas Cooper at the height of the disturbances of summer 1842, described one confrontation:

> My house has been surrounded with police these two nights and a warrant issued for my apprehension. I have nevertheless marched with the sovereign people, and addressed them in defiance of their warrant. There was some ugly work last night. My bodyguard chucked a raw lobster into the canal and the town has been paraded by soldiers, our lads cheering and marching with them like trumps.[36]

To the Chartists, the Leaguers and to politicians in general, 'the people' in 1842 were the working class. Is it possible, however, to see in the Chartist use of 'the people' a less restricted definition than that of those to whom it meant, effectively, working men? Historians in the nineteenth century tended to masculinize expressions like 'crowd' and 'movement', while the earliest labour historians tended to present 'class' as a basically masculine expression. In looking at some of the Chartist attitudes to women it may be possible to suggest that for some at least of the speakers and writers 'the people' included both sexes, and it is certainly clear that the female participation in Chartist activities was an aspect which surprised and shocked even some of those among the higher classes who were sympathetic to the movement.

In his speech in support of the Chartists' right to be heard at the Bar of the House of Commons, Duncombe found the number of women signatories to the petition something of an embarrassment. He described them as 'the signatures of a considerable portion of the wives of the industrious classes' and maintained that they, together with the signatures of young people below the age of twenty-one,

---

36. Quoted in Irving, *Annals of Our Time* p. 117; S. Roberts, *Radical Politicians and Poets in Early Victorian Britain* (New York, 1993), pp. 20–1.

demonstrated the support of the petition by whole families.[37] But the assumption that all female signatories were
wives or mothers of male Chartists does not square with the
admittedly few indicators we have of the occupations of
Chartist women. They seem to have included as well as
female members of Chartist families (who were in any case
often the instigators of radical ideas and activity) single
women such as servants, textile operatives, shopkeepers and
innkeepers as well as women housekeeping for other family
members. Women had been urged to join the National
Charter Association from its foundation, and their presence
at all the major demonstrations at least up until the
mid-1840s is well attested. In 1842 indeed there was probably a greater number of women actively participating in the
demonstrations and strikes than at any other period. For
John Bright, the women's actions were the first sign of real
revolt. He wrote to his brother-in-law: 'About 2000 women
paraded the town this morning, singing hymns. The men are
gone to other towns and villages to turn all the hands out.
Has the revolution commenced? It looks very probable. The
authorities are powerless.'[38] When the strikers marched into
Rochdale later the same day, they were headed by 'women,
eight or ten abreast, singing lively songs'. However, when
Bright decided to intervene by writing a letter to the strikers,
it was to the working *men* that he addressed himself.[39]
Eyewitness accounts of the summer of 1842 make the
participation of women in the demonstrations very clear. In
his book on the strikes, Mick Jenkins gives five pages of
episodes involving women, mainly from Lancashire and the
Potteries.[40] The Chartist crowd, like the workforce in the
manufacturing districts, included both sexes.

   Disraeli made not only the central character in his
Chartist novel *Sybil*, published in 1844 but based on
the events of 1842, a woman, but included women of the

   37. Hansard, LXIII, 3 May 1842.
   38. Quoted in J. Cole, *Conflict and Co-operation* (Littleborough,
1994), p. 32.
   39. Leech, *Public Letters*, pp. 334–40.
   40. M. Jenkins, *The General Strike of 1842* (London, 1980), pp. 213–17.

factory districts among the most political and argumentative of his Chartists. In the novel two kinds of working-class women are portrayed: the lively, independent factory girls, ardent Chartists, if anything more courageous than their male companions, ready to use any weapons, including sexual favours, to further the cause, and the miserable, exploited women of the mining and metal-working districts, beaten by their menfolk and exploited by grasping employers and by tommy and badger shops. Her Chartist father speaks regretfully of Sybil's talk of taking the veil, for 'the married life of a woman of our class in the present conditions of our country is a lease of woe ... Even woman's spirit cannot stand against it.'[41] Fortunately, Sybil turns out to have noble blood and so is able to make a good marriage, but one of the factory girls remains single and becomes a capitalist herself rather than surrender her independence by marrying. Disraeli was an astute observer and saw many things that were missed by less politically-minded novelists who dealt with the Chartists. In spite of the active participation of women, especially in the textile districts, Chartism never had a specifically female agenda; indeed quite contradictory statements can be heard, as they were later in the century within the women's movements.

In May 1842 the publication of the *First Report of the Children's Employment Commission* had a great effect on public opinion. The conditions in which women and children worked in the manufacturing districts provided ammunition for radical politics and for humanitarian campaigns. Many issues were involved in the attempts to regulate the labour of women and children. Working-class activists in the short time movement made no secret of the fact that they wanted a reduction of working hours for all, but it was easier to win support among middle- and upper-class philanthropists for a campaign to limit the hours of women and children. In many cases arguments for such a programme included not only a protest against the physical

---

41.   B. Disraeli, *Sybil* (London, 1954 edn.), pp. 136–7 and passim. This quotation has been slightly abbreviated.

exploitation of the weaker members of society, but arguments based on the destruction of the working-class family. Oastler was in a debtors' prison in 1842, put there by his former employer largely because of his activities in opposition to the 1834 Poor Law and his campaign against child labour in the factories. He published his journal the *Fleet Papers* from prison and conducted a running argument with the League on economic matters whilst also carrying on his campaign for factory reform. One of his most frequent accusations was that the factory employers, by always seeking the cheapest labour, fractured traditional family patterns by employing the women and children and leaving the men to care for the house and babies. In April 1842 he published extracts from the journal of the West Riding radical Mark Crabtree, who had just returned from a tour of the factory districts. Crabtree gave accounts of women working to support unemployed husbands and fathers. He also described the women's clubs that were spreading:

Female clubs are composed of a certain number of females (married and single), generally about fifty or sixty in number, who hold their meetings weekly at public houses. The ostensible purpose of these clubs is to protect each other from want in case of sickness, a provision also being made in case of death. These objects are laudable and praiseworthy, but, on a nearer view of the subject, we find evils attached to these clubs. It may easily be imagined what will be the consequence of fifty women meeting together in a public house and enjoying themselves in drinking, singing and smoking for two or three hours, and then being brought in contact with a number of men assembled in some other part of the house, the husbands waiting for their wives to go home and the young men through curiosity or worse intentions. Immediately after the breaking up of the club the women and men get intermixed in the tap room and other parts of the house and then commences a series of discourses of the lowest, most brutal and disgusting language imaginable; and if, as is sometimes the case, the

husbands should bethink themselves of the family at home
and urge the wife to depart, she will generally show signs of
vexation and insist on having her own way in these matters.
He, poor man, *well knowing that HIS livelihood depends
on HER labour*, is obliged to submit and quietly wait her
pleasure or go to his neglected children alone.[42]

It is more than probable that among the women in the clubs
of which Crabtree wrote were many of the 'hen radicals' at
whom the respectable papers jeered. These were the women
who were out on the streets in the factory districts and
throwing stones at soldiers in the Calder Valley.

There was certainly very much more talk about women's
rights and the possibility of women's suffrage among the
Chartists than in any other political discourse that was
around in England in 1842. Moreover, the idea was seen as
a challenge to the upper class. John La Mont, author of a
series of articles on the state of the Chartist movement in
1842, observed that it was time

> to suggest . . . such changes as the . . . extension of the
> suffrage to sane-minded males of eighteen years of age
> instead of twenty-one, already provided by our Charter;
> and the enfranchisement of females – notwithstanding the
> amount of blackguardism, folly and coercion which will be
> arrayed against this extension by the aristocratic
> debauches.[43]

In the same journal Elizabeth Neesom, who, with her
husband, ran a Chartist school in London in 1842, was
writing regularly against drink and tobacco. The two
voices – that of the independent working woman and that
of the woman defending the working-class family against

---

42. *Fleet Papers*, 9 April 1842.
43. *English Chartist Circular*, II, nos. 71–84. This Scottish Chartist
writer also contributed verse under the pseudonym 'Eugene La Mont' to the
Northern Star, 15 August, 26 September, 10 October 1840 and 11
September 1841; and to the *Chartist Circular*, 20 March, 31 July, 7 August,
18 September and 6 November 1841.

the factory system, the Poor Law and the drink trade can both be heard, though too often filtered through the observations of men or through the programmes of different reform campaigns. The arguments are not necessarily mutually exclusive, for the women's manifestoes which most clearly claimed political rights for women also complained of the 'soul- and body-degrading toil' to which women and their children were forced when their husbands' wages were inadequate or work was not available for men.

For many, if not most of the Chartists, 'the people' clearly did include not only men but also women and children. Among the extra-parliamentary radicals it may have had in this respect a different and wider meaning from that used by their opponents and supporters within the political system. Nevertheless the concept had clearly, in 1842, to be taken, in nearly every case, to mean working people or the working class. It was a divisive and never a unifying term.

4

WOMEN CHARTISTS

The first Reform Act of 1832 for the most part, satisfied those reformers who had gained admission to the franchise.[1] Since the 1832 franchise was clearly defined in terms of property, those who remained excluded had a very strong sense of the class nature of the Act's provisions. The Chartists considered that they were taking part in a working-class movement, and employed the language of class consistently throughout their campaigns. The fact that women were also excluded from the provisions of the 1832 Act did not lead to a specifically female agitation. Middle- and upper-class women seem to have been content with the extension of their class voice, or to have preferred to continue their more oblique methods of exerting influence on elections rather than associating themselves with those excluded on grounds of lack of property.

Insofar as a feminist claim for political rights was heard during the two decades after 1832, it was among the women and some men in the Chartist movement. For the most part, however, the many thousands of women who took part in

---

1. This essay was first published on the website Encyclopedia of the 1848 Revolutions, http://www.ohio.edu/chastain/rz/womchart.htm. The opening paragraph and the fifth paragraph have been abbreviated.

Chartism did so in support of a class programme or in opposition to specific acts of government. Women writers such as Charlotte Brontë, Elizabeth Gaskell and George Eliot who wrote about Chartism and radicalism in the period did not indicate any support for universal male and female suffrage. In the Chartist press and in pamphlets, however, both a general support for the vote for unmarried women was expressed and particular women's grievances were sometimes aired in association with a demand for political rights. For example, a letter from a Glasgow weaver in 1838 was addressed to her 'Fellow Countrywomen' and began:

> I address you as a plain working woman ... You cannot expect me to be grammatical in my expressions, as I did not get an education like many other of my fellow women that I ought to have got, and which is the right of every human being. It is the right of every woman to have a vote in the legislation of her country, and doubly more so now that we have got a woman at the head of government.[2]

The association of the accession of a young woman to the throne with the demand for women's admission to the political nation was heard on a number of occasions among the Chartists and was picked up on by Disraeli in *Sybil*, the only fictional treatment of Chartism which is sympathetic to the political demands of the movement or which recognizes the important part played in it by women.

Well over a hundred separate female Chartist associations are recorded in the period 1838–48.[3] For the most part, however, their activity and their programmes were supportive of male political demands or were insisting on their rights and their needs as family members. A slogan often repeated by men and women in the movement was 'No women's work except in the hearth and the

---

2. *Northern Star*, 23 June 1838.
3. See J. Schwarzkopf, *Women in the Chartist Movement* (London, 1991), pp. 199–217.

schoolroom'. The women's manifesto of Newcastle upon Tyne, a major port and an area with a great deal of women's work in glass-making and food-processing industries, expressed sentiments which often appeared:

> We have seen that because the husband's earnings could not support his family, his wife has been compelled to leave her home neglected and, with her infant children, work at soul- and body-degrading toil. For years we have struggled to maintain our homes in comfort, such as our hearts told us should greet our husbands after their fatiguing labours. Year after year has passed away, and even now our wishes have no prospect of being realized, our husbands are over-wrought, our houses half-furnished, our families ill-fed and our children uneducated.[4]

The activities which women initiated tended to be those which fitted the extension of their family roles. They embroidered banners, sashes and caps of liberty for speakers, organized tea parties and soirees to raise money or to entertain and honour leading figures, and took the leading role in setting up the many Chartist day and evening schools that were established for adults and children throughout the manufacturing districts. There were, however, other kinds of activity which might also be seen as to some extent traditional in which women took part which brought them into confrontation with the authorities in a more direct way. As family marketers, they often took the lead in organizing the boycott of shopkeepers who had shown hostility to Chartism or, conversely, in encouraging and patronizing those who used their vote or their influence to support the Chartists. The 1832 Reform Act had brought many fairly small traders into the voting strata, and, since some of these depended on working-class custom, this was a way in which the sheer number of small purchases made by working people could be used to influence at least a small part of the political action. In actual confrontations

---

4. *Northern Star*, 9 February 1839.

with the police or military such as occurred during the summer of 1842, there is ample evidence of women's presence among the demonstrators and rioters, throwing stones and providing ammunition by the apronful for male stone-throwers, or indulging in the traditional tactic of rough females in older societies of taunting the police or military, often with coarse or obscene language.[5]

The women Chartists were taking part in a community strategy, using in many cases traditional means of asserting hostility to measures such as the Poor Law Amendment Act of 1834, which was perceived as an attack on the working-class family. As the decade continued, the authorities responded in some ways – for example, the operation of the New Poor Law was modified in practice – and some of the crowd politics of the mass demonstration were abandoned in favour of a more 'modern' type of organization, the National Charter Association. Although there is evidence of the participation of many women in this organization, in general this kind of structure, which was to become the usual one as the modern labour movement developed, had less room for the unskilled, the migrant and the non-wage-earners among the working class. Changes in work patterns that also occurred during these years tended to take work out of the home and small workshop and away from family production. These factors seem to have lessened the active participation of women in popular politics which, like most aspects of public life in Britain, became largely 'masculinized' during the second half of the nineteenth century.

The masculinization of the movement that could be observed during the final years of Chartism also helps to explain the curious omission of Chartist women from most histories of the movement. Its early historians, both Fabian and Marxist, were concerned to present Chartism as a legitimate ancestor of the late-nineteenth-century labour political movements. In the atmosphere of those

---

5.   See A. Clark, *The Struggle for the Breeches: Gender and the Making of the British Working Class* (London, 1995), pp. 227–31.

years, however, the admission of the presence of women in the earlier movements would seem to have detracted from its seriousness and responsibility. The roughness of behaviour and the language of the Chartist women did not fit the image of the respectable nineteenth-century female, while the lack of a specifically feminist political programme meant they were of little interest to the feminist movement that arose in the later years of the century. In leaving out women from the history of Chartism, however, labour historians missed the important part played in this early working-class movement by family and community loyalties. Neither the massive popular demonstrations of the early years nor the support given to imprisoned and victimized leaders and their families would have been possible, had the movement not enjoyed the support of men and women in the manufacturing districts in which it flourished.

5

'THE QUESTION "WHAT IS A CHARTIST?" ANSWERED': CHARTIST TRACTS

GREG CLAEYS, *THE CHARTIST MOVEMENT IN BRITAIN 1838–1850* (2001)

Chartism held a unique place among the many movements for political reform that took place in Europe during the first half of the nineteenth century.[1] Two factors set it apart from the revolutionary activity that disturbed the national and imperial structures of continental Europe. The first of these was the constitutional shift that in 1832 admitted significant sections of the commercial and professional classes into British politics, who in most parts of Europe still felt themselves to be excluded from political power and so often provided the programmes and articulated the grievances of all those beyond the constitutional pale. The second was the fact that Britain, a rapidly urbanizing and a Protestant country, had a working population with a high level of literacy and habits of reading and discussing a range of texts.

When the 1832 Reform Act creamed off the main body of the politically-discontented middle class, the artisans and the labouring poor built their own reform movement from the strong-surviving tradition of lower-class radicalism and the long-standing traditions of Nonconformist

---

1. This essay was originally published in the *Times Higher Education Supplement*, 5 April 2002. This is a shortened version.

sects and communities, as well as from a lively culture of popular theatre and printed ballad sheets. The widespread movement whose membership and support lay almost entirely among the artisan and labouring portions of the community produced an enormous amount of published material of all kinds, and was to a large degree held together organizationally by print and by the potential provided by the possession of a national newspaper. The circulation of this newspaper, the *Northern Star*, was among the highest of any paper in Britain.[2] The sources for the recovery of the history of Chartism are therefore, to a much larger extent than with any earlier movement, printed sources.

The publishers of the present set of six volumes have made easily available items that are of concern to any student of nineteenth-century radical thought. All the items were originally published in the form of tracts or pamphlets, so there are no journal or manuscript sources among them. This is a collection that will enable students to make first-hand acquaintance with material that would otherwise be stacked away in libraries all over the country. It must be said, however, that the collection only goes part way towards defining the Chartist movement or extending the understanding of it. Manhood suffrage had been the aspiration of democratic politicians and political movements since classical times, and it is now so much a part of the definition of political democracy that modern readers may be puzzled by the repetition of the case for it or of the opposition to it. Fear of granting the right to vote to men of no property was widespread even among advanced Liberals in 1838, and so the arguments that many of the tracts in these volumes make, which were addressed primarily to an educated middle-class readership, were seen to be necessary and are indeed taken by the editor to indicate support for

---

2. J. Epstein, *The Lion of Freedom* (1982), p. 68, estimates that at its peak in 1839 sales of the *Star* reached 50,000 copies a week. Also see Thompson's contribution to J. Godechot, ed., *La Presse Ouvrière 1819–1850* (Paris, 1966).

Chartism. The Chartist movement, however, was not defined primarily by its programme, but, as Miles Taylor has argued, by the precise form in which it was presented at different times in the thirties and forties, and also by the nature and extent of its support. Chartism was in fact a political programme supported by a nationwide popular movement, demonstrated in massive gatherings, petitions whose signatories amounted to millions and a national press that was undoubtedly read by more people than any other in the country.[3] The founding in some districts of Chartist educational and cultural institutions have been seen by some historians as forming the basis for an alternative kind of community life.[4] The movement was not simply asking for change and improvement, but was also defending traditional and customary rights and practices. Thus, Richard Oastler, factory reformer, high churchman and opponent of manhood suffrage, was more popular with the Chartist crowd and more sympathetically treated in the Chartist press than Joseph Sturge or Richard Cobden, who favoured political reforms not far from the Chartist programme.

Many of the tracts in this collection were written by men who were not part of the Chartist movement, although they supported the main points of the Charter. Moreover, some of those writers who were important in the early days, including William Lovett and Bronterre O'Brien, are represented here not only by Chartist writing but by material that was written in years when they actively opposed mainstream Chartism. The National Association for Promoting the Political and Social Improvement of the People was set up in 1841 as an alternative to the National Charter Association at a time when Lovett was moving towards his later position of an educational qualification

3. M. Taylor, 'The Six Points: Chartism and the Reform of Parliament', in O. Ashton, R. Fyson and S. Roberts, eds, *The Chartist Legacy* (Rendlesham, 1999), pp. 1–23.

4. Perhaps the best example of a Chartist school is that founded by Thomas Cooper in Leicester: see S. Roberts, *The Chartist Prisoners* (Oxford, 2008), pp. 76–7.

for the vote. There is no evidence that the National Association or its publications were ever supported by the movement or any part of it.[5] The arguments put forward by Lovett after his imprisonment for Chartist activities, or by O'Brien in his later alternative organization or in his support for the Complete Suffrage Union of Sturge – from which even Lovett, by then very much opposed to Feargus O'Connor and the mainstream movement, withdrew – may have been better arguments than those of O'Connor, Peter Murray McDouall, William Cuffay and others.[6] It was these latter, however, who carried on the movement, organized the collection of signatures and the presentation of the petitions, who arranged and spoke at the demonstrations and who in, 1848, went to prison in the last big round-up of seditious leaders during the year of European revolutions.

Probably the most divisive moment in Chartism's history was the Newport rising of November 1839 and the subsequent transportation of its leaders. Surprisingly, these events get almost no mention in this collection. It was surely at this point that the division took place between those who feared the escalation of violence and those who, although rarely, if ever, advocating violent revolution, continued to support a programme of a massive demonstration of numbers. Sturge, a sincere supporter of the extension of the franchise and of religious toleration, was prepared to work only with selected leaders of the Chartists and under a name other than Chartist. This was the issue over which Lovett withdrew from collaboration with the CSU and over which O'Brien – who never joined the National Charter Association – lost most of his following. The introduction here seems to underestimate the power of loyalty to leaders who were seen as unquestionably committed to the movement and to have made sacrifices for it. This was a power

5.   See J. Weiner, *William Lovett* (London, 1989), pp. 83–9, 96–113.

6.   For McDouall see O. Ashton and P. A. Pickering, *Friends of the People: Uneasy Radicals in the Age of the Chartists* (London, 2002), pp. 7–28; for Cuffay, see Chase, *Chartism*, pp. 303–11.

that Major-General Charles Napier, the commander of the north in the Chartist years, recognized when he welcomed the commutation of the death sentences on the Newport leaders, since his experience in Ireland had taught him a lot about the charisma of martyrdom.

The introduction also misplaces the Land Company, and thereby fails to understand the power and energy that fuelled the movement. Unlike the Anti-Corn Law League's programme of settling supporters on freehold land, the Chartist plan did not create freeholds. Some of those who drew allotments may have had entitlement to vote by holding other freehold property, but the Chartist allotments were not freehold, nor was gaining the vote a motivation of the plan. O'Connor's idea, and that of his followers, was the creation of an alternative way of life by which industrial work and wages could be measured. Like most Irishmen of his time, O'Connor had strong attachment to the land and to an agrarian way of life and the scheme was to provide an escape from the traps set by the factory system and the 1834 Poor Law. A reading of Ernest Jones's journal, the *Labourer*, makes this clear and shows the powerful emotional and imaginative appeal that the Land Plan inspired. Again, it may well be argued that the idea was mistaken; but it was never a cold calculation of the achievement of a 40-shilling franchise.

There are many important texts in these six volumes. The original People's Charter, published in 1838 in the form of a detailed Act of Parliament to be presented to the House of Commons, appears early in volume one. This was not, however, the form in which the petition of 1839 was presented, when the demands did not include equal electoral districts, to which some of the Liberal supporters objected because of the possible massive influence of the Irish peasantry. This later version is not included in this collection. It would have been interesting to compare it to the petition of 1842 – in which the repeal of the 1834 Poor Law Amendment Act and the Act of Union were added to the programme – and to that of 1848, which was the only one to state the six points alone and to be supported in Parliament by a Chartist MP.[7]

The full report is published in volume three of the first Birmingham conference, held in April 1842, to found the Complete Suffrage Union. This gives readers the opportunity to study in some detail the problems of definition and rhetoric that students of Chartism face. Here a group of well-intentioned free trade advocates, many of them clergymen, set out to bring together the better parts of Chartism and the free trade movement. It is clear throughout the recorded discussions that tensions between the various speakers often expressed themselves in attitudes towards specific terms. John Collins, for example, who turned towards somewhat quietist Christianity after his imprisonment, spoke early in the discussion. 'And now, sir, you will allow me to observe that I think too much has been said against the class of which I have the honour to be one (I mean the working class) by those from whom better things might have been expected.' The question was taken up later by John Adam of Aberdeen, who 'thought the reference to "classes" injudicious. It should be their wish to put an end to that division into classes which had so much interfered with the progress of reform.'

Here we have encapsulated one of the divisions in the Chartist movement that had as much resonance at many important moments as the physical force–moral force dichotomy. The second Birmingham conference of December 1842 was to provide a dramatic illustration of the power of words when Lovett, already in disagreement with O'Connor and most of the other Chartist leaders, refused to relinquish the name Chartist, a name for which he and Collins had served terms of imprisonment. The tracts in these volumes enable readers to follow some of the differences of language and of narrative that can give many insights into the dynamics of the movement.[8]

---

7. S. Roberts, 'Feargus O'Connor in the House of Commons, 1847–55', in Ashton, Fyson and Roberts, *The Chartist Legacy*, pp. 102–118; Pickering, *Feargus O'Connor*, pp. 126–37.

8. A. Tyrell, *Joseph Sturge and the Moral Radical party in Early Victorian Britain* (London, 1987), pp. 124–31; Roberts, *The Chartist Prisoners*, pp. 65–7.

These volumes are full of important and interesting material, but because they are restricted to tracts, they do not include examples of the most lively Chartist statements that are to be found in the newspapers, broadsheets and reports of speeches – sympathetic reports in their own journals, and hostile ones in London and provincial papers and in police and spies' reports. The plays, the jokes, comic songs and hymns that gave life and colour to the movement are not to be found here, nor much in the way of personal accounts that were to appear later in the century. It is a collection that stresses the serious side of the movement, the problems that middle-class sympathizers had with supporting its programme and, above all, the continuing argument for adult male suffrage aimed at those former reformers who agreed with Lord John Russell ('Finality Jack' to the Chartists) that the 1832 Reform Act had signified the finality of parliamentary reform.[9]

---

9. See J. Belchem, *Labour History Review* 67:2 (2002), 248–50, for another interesting discussion of this collection.

6

CHARTIST AUTOBIOGRAPHIES

DAVID VINCENT, ED. *TESTAMENTS OF RADICALISM: MEMOIRS OF WORKING CLASS POLITICIANS 1790–1885* (1977)

The study of popular history is self-evidently beset by the great difficulty of recovering the experience of the less influential and less articulate members of society.[1] Not that this difficulty has prevented the publication of a great many confident statements about the beliefs and attitudes of the lower orders. One of the many myths in this area is the suggestion that literacy was brought to the lower orders by the advent of a state-supervised national system of elementary education, and that before this arrived working people were illiterate, superstitious, drunken, prone to irrational and riotous forms of behaviour, and easy meat for every false messiah or demagogue who offered himself. Mark Hovell described the supporters of the campaign against the New Poor Law as 'ignorant and unlettered men . . . coarsened by evil surroundings and brutalized by hard and unremitting toil, relieved only by periods of unemployment in which their dull minds brooded over their misfortunes'.[2] Subsequent scholarship made progress towards the recovery of the values shared by the working communities of the

---

1. This essay was originally published in the *Times Literary Supplement*, 18 November 1977. This is a slightly shortened version.
2. M. Hovell, *The Chartist Movement* (Manchester, 1966 edn.), p. 86.

early nineteenth century, showing them to be a more consistent system of values and beliefs than had earlier been allowed for. It has shown, moreover, that important shifts in attitudes and behaviour that undoubtedly occurred in the first half of the nineteenth century cannot simply be attributed to the filtering downwards of rather vaguely defined 'middle-class attitudes', but can be seen to have occurred within the working-class communities themselves. One of the manifestations of a change from an episodic, picaresque way of living to a more planned and apparently rational way was the development of national organizations within a permanent institutional structure.

Among the working class, trade unions, friendly societies and political organizations took on this more formal shape in the middle decades of the nineteenth century. It should be noted, however, that in political terms at any rate, a formal national structure occurred earlier among working-class radicals than among the traditional political parties, and that such organization owed nothing to middle-class encouragement or example. So far from national education preceding the growth of a working-class press and the spread of working-class literacy, it could be argued that the support which the movement for a national system achieved in the 1830s and 1840s was largely a response to working-class radicalism rather than to working-class illiteracy. The correspondence files of the National Society contain little reference to the horrors of illiteracy, but a great deal to the evils of Owenism, Chartism and infidelity.

The autobiographies reprinted in this excellent book form part of the evidence from which a picture of working-class radicalism in the early decades of the nineteenth century can be built. They contain also valuable clues to a greater understanding of other aspects of working-class life of the time, although the accent is very much on the political experience of their authors. By the time Benjamin Wilson was writing in the 1880s, the Liberal improving ideology had taken over and he tended to see all movements away from the old society as 'improvement'.

Such nostalgia as surfaced in his writing did so in spite of himself. Although Wilson's account of his youthful Chartism is one of the most valuable documents available for the study of the movement, a reading of it reminds us that the best account of radicalism in a manufacturing district is still that of Samuel Bamford, with his ear for the speech and the songs of the district and his ability to write about the same people at work and at leisure as well as engaged in political activity.[3]

Like all historical documents, these life-stories must be used with caution and an awareness of the precise context in which they were written. With this proviso, they remain a vivid and personal way of entering into the events which they describe. They vary greatly as narratives in length, in style and in manner. Wilson, Halifax labourer and gardener, and John James Bezer, Spitalfields snob, present themselves as small sections of the great crowd who made up the Chartist movement, and are at their best when they are giving a worm's-eye view of the great events in which they took part.[4] James Watson and Thomas Dunning were not among the top leadership of their movements, but leaders who took crucial initiatives at certain times.[5] Dunning, the Nantwich shoemaker, and Bezer are stylists: Bezer in

---

3. S. Bamford, *Passages in the Life of a Radical* (Middleton, 1839–41). Also see M. Hewitt and R. Poole, eds, *The Diaries of Samuel Bamford* (Stroud, 2000).

4. Bezer was imprisoned for two years for sedition in 1848. His autobiography was never completed. See K. Mays, 'Subjectivity, Community and the Nature of Truth-Telling in Two Chartist Autobiographies', in Ashton, Fyson and Roberts, *The Chartist Legacy*, pp. 196–231.

5. James Watson (1799–1874), a Yorkshireman, was well known in London radical circles from the early 1820s. He was imprisoned for blasphemy (1823) and, on two occasions, for selling unstamped publications (1833 and 1834–35). He worked closely with William Lovett, helping draw up the People's Charter. A printer and publisher, he brought out a number of small late Chartist journals, including Harney's *Democratic Review*. He never gave up on the radical cause. Thomas Dunning (1813–94), a shoemaker, organized Chartist and trade union activities in Nantwich. He was the local agent for the *Star*, and led working people into vestry meetings to protest against church rates. In the 1850s and 1860s he wrote regularly for the *Chester Record*. See C. Godfrey, *Chartist Lives*, pp. 495–6, 552–3.

particular, whose Cockney gabble jumps off the page, punning, allusive, lapsing constantly into humorous dialogue. Dunning is more straightforward, but with the occasional telling phrase – 'Bayley could read and write a little, but he was a light-minded, dancing public house man' – and off-beat detail – 'I visited him in prison, lent him a flute to amuse himself . . . and advised him not to allow himself to be bound over'.[6] Dunning's whole account of how the shoemakers of Nantwich frustrated a criminal prosecution within a few months of the Tolpuddle labourers' case is cool and humorous, but conveys a sense of imminent menace.

Much can be learnt from these, and from others among the surprisingly large number of autobiographies which have survived from these years.[7] One thing they demonstrate, as David Vincent points out in his perceptive introduction, is the extent to which the radicalism of the first half of the nineteenth century was a matter of the whole working community, men and women, and not of isolated groups or sects. Another is the rational behaviour of these radicals, often in contrast to the behaviour of their betters. James Watson, for instance, served two sentences of imprisonment, once for defying the Newspaper Stamp Act, a measure deliberately imposed to prevent the circulation of cheap printed journals, the other for defying a national day of fasting, called by the government to appease the deity who had visited London with a cholera epidemic. Watson and his fellow prisoners Lovett and William Benbow had

---

6. 'Reminiscences of Thomas Dunning', in D. Vincent, ed., *Testaments of Radicalism*, p. 129. Matthew Bayley had been arrested in August 1834 for being a member of an unlawful combination and for administering illegal oaths; the second quotation refers to another individual arrested on the same charge, Robert Edwards. The prosecution was eventually abandoned.

7. J. Burnett, D. Mayall and D. Vincent, eds, *The Autobiography of the Working Class: An Annotated Critical Bibliography* (Brighton, 1984) lists thirty-six autobiographies written by Chartists. E. Griffin, *Liberty's Dawn: A People's History of the Industrial Revolution* (New Haven, CT, 2013), examines working class autobiographies from a new angle: see pp. 212–40 for her discussion of the Chartists.

organized a march through London followed by a feast for poorer members of their association, believing that deaths from cholera were more likely to be caused by malnutrition among the poor than by divine wrath.[8] Thomas Dunning recounts the experience of perjured evidence and rigged trials, while Bezer gives a hilarious account of the antics of the Mendicity Society, who succeed in giving free bread-and-cheese dinners to the most degraded and dishonest of London's professional beggars, while brutally snubbing the only honest man innocent enough to accept their promises.

Enough is supplied of notes and introduction to make *Testaments of Radicalism* clear to any reader. Stylistic and grammatical idiosyncrasies are retained, giving a slight regional flavour to some of the writing, which is, of course, mercifully free from the patronizing which mars a great deal of 'oral history' of working people. The editor and publishers are to be congratulated on bringing together in a handy and accessible form these works which, although not unknown or unpublished, have become difficult to get hold of in their older forms. They are apologias for the lives of a group of radical activists. The reader may not accept them, but he cannot doubt their authenticity.

---

8. Weiner, *William Lovett*, pp. 28–30. London radicals termed the fast on 21 March 1832 'Farce Day'; Lovett, Watson and Benbow were arrested after police broke up a procession but acquitted in May of unlawful assembly.

II

A LOCAL STUDY

The first essay in this section is not, as might be assumed, a discussion of Chartism in manufacturing centres in the West Riding or Lancashire. It is instead a commentary on how such research could be undertaken by local historians. As a clarion call for research into Chartist localities, it is an overlooked contribution to the historiography of the movement. The essay includes some interesting early observations about the sources that could be used in writing about the Chartists.

Dorothy and Edward Thompson were at the time working on an essay on Chartism in their adopted town of Halifax. The essay was intended for, but did not appear in, *Chartist Studies* (1959), edited by Asa Briggs. It seems that the essay was originally commissioned by Briggs from Edward Thompson, but it is clearly a joint enterprise. Though the typescript does not identify either of them by name, there are phrases in the footnotes which confirm the collaboration, such as 'we accept . . .' and 'in our possession . . .'. There are jokes and expressions ('economic parasitism', 'the long agony', etc.) in the essay that are recognizably Edward's, but the fact that Dorothy subsequently made handwritten amendments to the typescript – though a number of later paragraphs and footnotes remained unfinished – and chose to deposit it with her own collection of books on Chartism in Staffordshire University Library, points to her as having written a sizeable part of the essay. Dorothy was especially interested at this time in Ernest Jones and the later phase of Chartism, and it seems very likely that she wrote a large part, though not all, of the essay from the strikes of 1842 onwards. The essay very much links political action with economic hardship, and is shot through with a deep sympathy for the plight of the weavers and combers of Halifax. Dorothy and Edward Thompson's deep admiration for the Chartist stalwart Ben Rushton, who they clearly regarded as a fine type of working-class leader, is made clear – as is Dorothy's fondness for Jones. John Snowden, a local leader who defected to the middle-class reformers in the 1850s, is castigated, and the mill owners such as Jonathan Akroyd are presented with disdain.

The typescript, which Briggs rejected, is unpolished and of considerable length. Edward, in particular, struggled to edit his own work. For all that, the essay remains a superb investigation into a Chartist stronghold. It is based on a very wide range of sources – autobiographies, local and Chartist newspapers, material in the Home Office – and has a very clear, and very Thompsonian, line of argument, emphasising the insurrectionary character of Halifax Chartism. Though other accounts of Halifax Chartism have been written, this essay still deserves to be enjoyed today.

7

CHARTISM IN THE
INDUSTRIAL AREAS

The history of Chartism has been written more than once from national sources.[1] There were a sufficient number of documents in the British Library and the Home Office Papers for the first historians of Chartism to be able to draw a fairly full picture of the movement as it appeared to the authorities in London.[2] It should be mentioned that a series of local studies, mainly of industrial centres, is in preparation under the editorship of Professor Asa Briggs of Leeds University. Nevertheless more work remains to be done on the local history of Chartism. One example of the sort of problem on which more light is needed is the well-known division in the movement between the exponents of 'moral force' and 'physical force'. That such a division existed amongst the leadership is very clear from the proceedings of the National Convention of 1839 and from the writings of the movement's chief journalists (who have often mistakenly been assumed to have been the most influential leaders). However, a study of some local groups in the West Riding, for example, suggests that, although

---

1.   This essay was first published in *Amateur Historian*, III, (1956), pp. 13–19. This is a shortened version.

2.   For example, J. West, *A History of the Chartist Movement* (London, 1920).

different views on the subject were held, these did not prevent their holders from working amicably together, however much their leaders may have been quarrelling.

What is one to look for in trying to piece together the story in a particular locality? It is clear that the three main periods of activity around the National Petitions of 1839, 1842 and 1848 differed in various ways. These differences become accentuated when a small area is studied, and one of the first points of interest to be established is the level of activity in the area under consideration at these different times. It is also important to note that, although these were the high peaks of national activity, there may have been local outbursts at different times. The second kind of information relates to the form of the Chartists' activities. These varied considerably from place to place as well as from time to time, and ranged from monster meetings and demonstrations to regular Sunday services with Chartist hymns and sermons, and from torchlight drilling to education classes and choirs. The extent to which Chartists took part in non-political demonstrations such as strikes or agitation for the relief of unemployment varied very much. Local industrial conditions were the determining factor here. In some areas they published their own newspapers and pamphlets and in most areas placards and leaflets. Nearly every important industrial area in the country had some record of Chartist electoral activity, either at the hustings or actually at the poll. An important form of activity about which little is known in most districts is the participation by Chartists in local elections after 1848.[3]

---

3. In 1852 Julian Harney and Samuel Carter appeared on the hustings as Chartist candidates in, respectively, Bradford and Tavistock. Harney, to his dismay, failed to win the show of hands; Carter was elected but, lacking the required property qualification, was soon unseated. Two interesting examples of Chartists who became elected councillors are John Collins of Birmingham and George Holloway (1818–1904) of Kidderminster. Collins was returned as a councillor for Ladywood in 1847; but his attempts to restrain council expenditure proved short-lived when the following year he was incapacitated by a stroke. By turns a carpet weaver, a dyer, a publican and a grocer, Holloway served as secretary and treasurer of the Kidderminster Chartists. Known as 'Honest George', he was, with only a

Having discovered the periods of the greatest activity, and the sort of activity which the local Chartists arranged, the next thing is to gather information about the personalities involved. Who were the local leaders? What were their jobs? How far were they representative of the chief industries of the town? Who were the people who really led the movement? Were they the major national figures who occasionally made visits? Were they local men whose names were little known outside their own towns? Or were the most influential men those intermediate people who did not own newspapers or have already established names outside Chartism, but who became very well-known as travelling missionaries and organizers, e.g. John West and George White?[4] What part did women play in the local organization? The answers to these questions will inevitably vary from place to place.

As well as finding out about the Chartists themselves, it is worth asking: who were their allies? Here, perhaps, will be found some of the biggest differences between localities. In the woollen areas, whilst some Tories were sympathetic, the Whigs were hostile. In the cotton towns, however, some sections of the Liberal manufacturers saw the Chartists as possible allies in their fight against the Corn Laws. Such alignments of sympathy varied very much from place to place, but there was certainly not a uniform attitude to Chartism on the part of the established parties. Indeed in the 1847 election, when O'Connor was returned in coalition with the Tory candidate at Nottingham, Ernest Jones secured a sizeable vote in coalition with the radical

---

few short breaks, a Liberal councillor from 1853 until his death. A number of Chartist councillors were also elected to town councils in the West Riding. For Holloway, see L. Smith, *Carpet Weavers and Carpet Masters* (Kidderminster, 1986), pp. 248–51.

4. West (1811–87) and White (1812–68) were Irishmen, arriving in England in the 1820s. In 1842–44 West was employed by the NCA as a lecturer in Yorkshire and in 1848 he was imprisoned (with White). A real thorn in the side of the authorities, White frequently found himself in a prison cell: his story is told in Roberts, *Radical Politicians and Poets in Early Victorian Britain*, pp. 11–38.

Edward Miall, editor of the *Nonconformist*.[5] As well as political allies, there were usually tradesman who found it profitable to sympathize with Chartism – most centres had at least one Chartist pub, and often a Chartist grocer and butcher as well.[6] Such tradesmen found their sympathies well rewarded when the non-electors practised 'exclusive dealing', which was common at election times.

The final point of interest to look out for in the local movement is the connection between Chartism and other movements. This can be particularly well shown in a local study where it is often possible to see the connections in terms of individuals. The ten hours movement, the anti-Poor Law movement and the early trade unions were sometimes sources from which local leaders drew their experiences.[7] During and after the Chartist period they worked to found co-operative societies, working men's clubs, educational and temperance societies, and branches of the Reform League. Nor should the connection with Nonconformist groups be overlooked. A number of local Chartist leaders were recruited from the ranks of Methodist lay preachers.[8]

---

5. See Roberts, 'Feargus O'Connor in the House of Commons', in Ashton, Fyson and Roberts, *The Chartist Legacy*, pp. 104–7; C. Binder, 'The Nottingham electorate and the election of the Chartist, Feargus O'Connor, in 1847', in *Transactions of the Thoroton Society* 107 (2003), 145–62.

6. For example, the publican of the Six Bells in Braintree, Essex, provided copies of the *Star* and local Chartists regularly met there. The Freeman's Inn in Barnsley, run by Peter Hoey (1807–75), also served as a meeting place for Chartists; Hoey lost the use of a leg during his imprisonment in 1840–41. For Hoey, see C. Godfrey, *Chartist Lives*, pp. 509–11.

7. For example, R. J. Richardson of Salford was secretary of the South Lancashire Anti-Poor Law Association; William Aitken (1814–69) of Ashton-under-Lyne testified before the Royal Commission on Child Labour in 1833; and Christopher Doyle (1811–?) of Manchester was imprisoned, in 1837, for leading a strike of power-loom weavers. All three men spent time in prison in 1840. For Aitken, see R. G. Hall and S. Roberts, eds, *William Aitken: The Writings of a Nineteenth-Century Working Man* (Tameside, 1996).

8. For example, John Goslin (dates unknown) of Ipswich, W. V. Jackson (1803–?) of Manchester and Ben Rushton (1785–1853) of Halifax were former Methodist preachers. Jackson was one of the most popular Chartist preachers in Lancashire.

The starting point for research into Chartism is the *Northern Star*. A complete file of this newspaper is preserved in the British Library, but few actual copies have survived elsewhere. The great majority of readers of the *Star*, as for all other Chartist journals, were working-class, and the houses in which they lived, and in which they might possibly have left newspapers, have long since been destroyed. In any case there is much less likelihood of newspapers being kept in small houses than large, and certainly very little chance of their being bound. The great mass therefore of newspapers, pamphlets, minute books and other records belonging to the Chartists have long since been destroyed. The *Star* has the very great merit, for our purposes, of always printing full reports of local activity when these were sent in. It had its own reporters in certain large towns, and many of the main national speakers and missionaries were in the habit of sending reports of their speeches and meetings.[9] But, in the main, the amount of space devoted to any particular locality depended on the energy of the local secretary in sending in reports of its meetings. Thus, for example, more is heard of the Barnsley group than of many others because Frank Mirfield sent in regular reports of their meetings and of resolutions passed.[10]

In the Home Office papers most of the reports on Chartism are filed according to counties – although here again there is no consistency in the manner of reporting. It seems that the fullness or otherwise of the descriptions of the events depended very much on the initiative of local magistrates and of other local citizens who felt it necessary to inform the Home Office of what was happening. Amongst the accounts are included a number of pamphlets,

---

9.   Harney, White and Thomas Martin Wheeler (1811–62) were paid correspondents for the *Star* in, respectively, Sheffield, Birmingham and London in the early 1840s.

10.   Frank Mirfield (1801–69) embraced Chartism on returning to Barnsley after being transported, and later pardoned, for leading a weavers' strike in 1829. He was again to lead a weavers' strike in 1843–44 and regularly chaired Chartist meetings. See C. Godfrey, *Chartist Lives*, pp. 520–1.

placards etc. sent from different places and some of these
are of very great interest and value. Odd copies of this sort
of material also survives in libraries. It is unfortunate that
only a relatively limited number of these are still in existence, as often they seem to have been published when a
local group was in disagreement with national policy or
when they were at loggerheads with the local press.

Local newspapers vary so much from place to place that
it is impossible to generalize as to their value. Some appear
to have been published all through the Chartist period
without a single reference to it. Others devote many
columns to it at peak periods. Some are so fiercely hostile
and derisory that their reports, though of great interest,
cannot be relied on as to their accuracy. The political
sympathies of the newspaper are, of course, of the greatest
importance and must be taken into account in assessing its
reports, but here again the mid-century alignments are
often confusing. A paper which stood for franchise reform
and free trade might be very hostile to Chartism whilst a
Tory paper like the *Halifax Guardian*, which had been
well-disposed to the ten hours movement, could be more
sympathetic, although, of course, fundamentally hostile to
the aims of Chartism. Later in the nineteenth century, when
Liberalism and free trade were triumphant, it became a
popular custom for local newspapers to publish reminiscences of the bad old days. Many of the most interesting
recollections of the Chartist period can be found amongst
such reminiscences.[11]

During the periods of greatest activity representatives of
most of the centres of Chartism found themselves in the
dock – at the magistrates' court, at quarter sessions or at the
assizes. The records of these courts, and the published
accounts of trials, should be scanned. Where reported, the
magistrates' comments are of interest, for they are sometimes
surprisingly sympathetic and often contain some remark
about the superior character of the Chartist prisoners.

---

11. See, for example, Arthur O'Neill in the *Birmingham Daily Post* in
1885 and W. H. Chadwick in the *Bury Times* in 1894.

'THE DIGNITY OF CHARTISM': HALIFAX AS A CHARTIST CENTRE (WITH E. P. THOMPSON)

I.

'Our borough of Halifax is now brightening into the polish of a large, smoke-canopied commercial town', Miss Lister, owner of Shibdon Hall, noted ironically in her diary in March 1837.[1] Head of an old and influential family, owning land, mines and property in the town and environs, her resentment against the March of Progress reminds us that Halifax was no mushroom-growth of the early nineteenth century. The upper Calder Valley, once the classic site of the domestic industry recorded by Daniel Defoe, was a stronghold of the small clothier well into the century. In Halifax there had been built the last of the West Riding 'Piece Halls', at which the stuff manufacturers still attended in Chartist times. The plentiful supply of water in the parish had delayed the introduction of steam, while scores of small masters established little water-powered spinning mills in the outlying cloughs and deans. Drouth in the 1820s speeded the introduction of steam; larger mills were built in the main valley bottom alongside the Rochdale canal; the

---

1. Extract from the diaries of Anne Lister, *Halifax Guardian*, August 1891. There has been much interest in Lister's extensive diaries in which she describes in detail her same-sex relationships. See H. Whitbread, ed., *The Secret Diaries of Miss Anne Lister* (2010).

advancing worsted industry became concentrated in fewer hands. From the large enterprises of such people as the Akroyd family there came much of the smoke and the 'polish'.

The parish of Halifax in 1831 was the largest in England, stretching from Brighouse in the east to the Lancashire border at Todmorden seventeen miles to the west, and taking in a large upland population alongside the Calder and its tributary, the Ryburn. The population of the parish was close on 110,000, although the rapidly-growing town-ship made up only 15,000 of this figure. 'A great proportion of its population', said an eyewitness in 1829, 'is not like that of Leeds, employed in the warp and woollens, nor in stuffs, as at Bradford, or fancy goods, as at Huddersfield or cottons, as at Manchester, but its trade is a mixture of all these combined.'[2]

The parish contained by far the largest concentration of the cotton industry in Yorkshire; while Halifax was second only to Bradford as a centre of the rapidly expanding worsted industry. A return of mills in the parish in 1831 shows fifty-seven cotton, thirty-five woollen, forty-five worsted and four silk, employing in all above 18,000 juve-nile adult workers. A further return in 1838 shows eighty worsted and sixty-three woollen mills, seventy-one cotton and seven silk.[3] While many of these were small and inse-cure ventures, large-scale enterprises were emerging, notably that of Jonathan Akroyd and his son Edward (employing, in 1845, 6,400 workers inside and outside his mills) and that of the Crossley brothers, whose first large carpet mill at Dean Clough was built in 1841. By the boom year of 1850 over 15,000 workers were employed within the walls of the parish worsted mills alone.[4]

---

2. *Halifax Courier & Guardian Almanac*, 1894, p. 93.
3. J. Crabtree, *A Concise History of the Parish and Vicarage of Halifax* (London, 1836), pp. 308–9; *Parliamentary Gazeteer*, (London, 1841), p. 234; J. James, *History of the Worsted Manufacture in England* (London, 1957), pp. 619–20.
4. *Halifax Guardian*, 10 May 1845; H. Forbes, *Rise, Progress & Present State of the Worsted Manufactures of England* (London, 1852),

Underneath the gathering canopy of smoke, there was to be found the same 'polish' as in other West Riding towns. Children comprised nearly one third of the labour force within the mills of the parish in 1835, and one half of the labour force of the borough in 1850. The Halifax masters were among the most intransigent and uninhibited opponents of factory legislation. Wages, even in the new power-loom sheds, were low. 'One man told me, with tears in his eyes, that he had been four weeks (six days in a week, and twelve hours a day) in earning 19s 6d at weaving with the power-loom', William Dodd, the 'Factory Cripple', noted. 'Formerly he could earn upwards of 20s a week by hand.' While some restraining influences were to be found in the township and immediate environs, the outlying districts and remoter valleys exhibited the blackest vices of early industrialization. Page after page of Frances Trollope's *Michael Armstrong: Factory Boy* (1840) might well have been drawn from such an isolated place as Cragg Vale, whose mill owners were 'the pest and disgrace of society . . . They say, "Let the Government make what laws they think fit"; they can drive a coach and six through them in that valley.' Here the abuses of truck were carried to extremes. 'What say the shopkeepers of Rochdale about you?' demanded Richard Oastler. 'Why, when they have stuff that they can't sell to anybody else, they say to their apprentices, "Lay it aside for the Cragg Dale manufacturers to sell to their work people." Why, you stink over Blackstone Edge!'[5]

Whilst in the Mytholm and Colden silk mills the *New Moral World* circulated and socialist utopias were eagerly

p. 318; R. Gray, *The Factory Question and Industrial England 1830–1860* (Cambridge, 1996), pp. 13–15, 24–5, 106–7.

5. W. Ranger, *Report on a Preliminary Inquiry as to the Sewerage, Drainage and Supply of Water and the Sanitary Conditions of Halifax* (London, 1851), p. 15; W. Dodd, *The Factory System Illustrated* (London, 1842), p. 150; G. Crabtree, *A Brief Description of a Tour Through Calderdale* (London, 1833); *Voice of the West Riding*, 20 July 1833; E. P. Thompson, *The Making of the English Working Class* (London, 1963), pp. 382–3.

debated, the strength of Chartism in the parish was to be drawn not in the first place from the mills but from the thousands of handworkers – weavers, combers and others – who entered their long agony at the beginning of the decade. In 1832 William Cobbett found the weavers of the valley to be 'extremely destitute': where they had formerly earned 20s to 30s a week, now they were reduced to 5s or less. 'It is the more sorrowful to behold these men in this state', he wrote, 'as they still retain the frank and bold character formed in the days of their independence.'[6] As the decade dragged on, continued parliamentary attention served only to keep alight among the weavers a glimmer of hope of legislative assistance and to bring redoubled bitterness when their desperate plight in the 1840s was met with nothing more than expressions of regret. The majority of them were now living on the edge of starvation, subsisting on oatcakes, skim milk and potatoes. Their cottages were often insanitary, decaying and bare of furnishings. The upland hamlets, from the debility of the population, were as subject to epidemics as the slums of the town. 'How they contrive to exist at all', exclaimed a surgeon who had visited the weavers' cottages at times of childbirth and sickness, 'confounds the very faculties of eyes and ears.'[7]

The yeoman clothier of Defoe's time had either – like the founder of the Akroyd fortune – prospered as a manufacturer, or been reduced to the status of a handloom weaver. The increased output of yarn from the spinning mills had led to a brief period of prosperity for the weavers, and an influx of labour into the trade. While in Halifax some manufacturers – notably in the carpet industry – employed handloom weavers on their own premises, the great majority of weavers outside the township worked in their own

---

6. *Cobbett's Political Register*, 30 January 1832.
7. A Select Committee was appointed, issuing reports in 1834 and 1835. These raised hopes by recommending a form of minimum wage, periodically reviewed in each district. A Royal Commission was appointed in 1837. Assistant commissioners toured the districts in 1838, their reports being published in 1839 and 1840. R. Howard, *History of the Typhus of Heptonstall-Slack 1843–4* (Hebden Bridge, 1844).

homes, sometimes owning their looms, sometimes paying rent for loom and tackle, and living in perpetual indebtedness to their employers. Manufacturers, master spinners, or intermediate factors put out the yarn among the weavers, paying them for the labour of the various weaving processes when the piece was finished.

The weaver was not an independent craftsman but a wage-labourer, working (like most outworkers) in exceptionally vulnerable conditions. His whole family employed – his children winding bobbins, his wife sometimes at a second loom – he had no regularity of employment, had to meet his own overheads (rent, candles, sizing etc.), was subject to fines for spoilt work, and received no payment for time spent in fetching and carrying his work, setting up his loom, and a dozen other processes. His wages were beaten down by successive competing employers, the least scrupulous or least successful setting the pace. The employer was liable to no overheads, and need fear no costs of idle plant during bad trade; he need only put out more or less yarn according to the state of the market. The degradation of the weavers was not caused by, but antedated, the widespread introduction of the power loom; and, indeed, so far from the power loom being the first cause of the weavers' suffering, the slowness of the introduction of the power into the worsted and (even slower) into the woollen industry, may be attributed in part to the cheapness of labour by hand. Correspondingly, the exploitation of the handworkers contributed to the debasing of wages in the power-loom sheds. As the mills continued to draw upon women and children for a high proportion of their labour force, the adult men – without prospect of employment – preferred to find occasional work in the relatively unskilled trades of weaver or comber to the alternatives of total unemployment. Hence these two trades represent in the Chartist period an enormous pool of disguised unemployment in the parish.

The entry of the power-loom weavers served to bring the long agony to a crisis in the 1840s. Coming first into cotton (and affecting especially the coarse fustian trade carried on extensively in the upper Calder Valley), it threw more handlooms onto the support of the worsted and woollen industries. In 1827 James Akroyd built the first large worsted power-loom shed in Halifax and introduced the Jacquard loom. Ten years later the firm opened its Hayley Hill mill, the largest in the worsted industry of the time.[8] By 1850 there were 4,000 power looms in the worsted industry in the parish.[9] Meanwhile the power loom was being rapidly improved in efficiency. But the hand weaver was not presented with a head-on contest with the machine as the hand comber was to be in the early 1850s. Rather, there was a complex series of repercussions within an industry whose total output was increasing by leaps and bounds over the whole period.[10] Forced out of cotton, facing severe competition with power in the worsted industry, the handloom was still the mainstay of the fancy woollen and carpet industries.[11] Indirectly power competition served to intensify the exploitation of the weavers in these industries as well, by flooding the remaining markets with labour. But this delayed and uneven development helps to explain the extreme tenacity of the weavers' generation-long struggle with starvation, which coincides with the rise and decline of the Chartist movement.

The worsted weavers of the district bitterly resented the introduction of power, demanding legislative restrictions

---

8. S. C. Moore, *Evolution of Industry in the Sowerby Division* (London, 1913), p. 15; *History of the Firm of James Akroyd & Son* (London, 1874), p. 13; J. James, *History of the Worsted Manufacture in England* (London, 1857), pp. 618–20.

9. See *Leeds Times*, 28 March, 11 April 1835, for estimates that the power-loom weaver could then produce up to three times as much work in a week as a handloom weaver. According to H. Forbes, *Rise, Progress & Present Day State of the Worsted Manufactures of England*, p. 318, the speed of shuttle movements on a mix-quarter loom more than doubled between 1839 and 1852.

10. Consumption of wool in the Halifax worsted industry: 1830, 3,657,000 lbs; 1850, 14,423,040 lbs.

11. Problems of applying the power loom effectively to carpets were only overcome in 1851. But the Crossley Carpet Power-Loom, patented on the last day of the year, could weave twelve to fourteen times the speed of hand. See *Halifax Courier*, 7 July 1888.

upon its use. If trade-union combination had been next to impossible before, in a scattered cottage industry riddled with variations of prices and practices, it was now out of the question. But – even if the weavers had not had strong traditional and moral objections to factory discipline and the factory system – age, inadaptability and lack of alternative employment prevented their absorption into other occupations.[12] Their spokesman Ben Rushton – who was to become the most notable of Halifax Chartist leaders – declared their condition in 1835 to be 'so ruinous that, if matters are suffered to go on as they have done, and are doing . . . that useful body will very soon be annihilated, or they must degenerate into paupers, poachers or thieves.'[13] Under Rushton's leadership, they became Chartists instead.

The plight of the hand woolcombers was little different. Wage labourers, some working in small workshops, some in their own houses, they had pioneered trade unionism in the worsted industry. While Bradford was the centre of trade unionism, Halifax took second place, and many Halifax combers (as well as worsted workers) had taken part in the long strike of 1825.[14] From this year forward their decline set in apace, although serious competition from combing machines did not come before the 1840s. Working and living in cramped quarters, amidst charcoal fumes from the comb pot, their poor health and short span of life was a subject for frequent comment. Frank Peel described them as 'almost without exception rabid politicians . . . The Chartist movement had no more enthusiastic adherents than these men; the *Northern Star* was their one book of study.'[15] The swift introduction of improved combing machines after 1845 brought matters to a sudden crisis, although in Halifax the final extinction of the hand combers was delayed until 1856 when Edward Akroyd,

---

12. See J. Fielden, *The Curse of the Factory System* (London, 1836), pp. 67–9.
13. *Leeds Times*, 11 April 1835.
14. J. Burnley, *Wool and Woolcombing* (London, 1889), pp. 159–85.
15. *Cleckheaton Guardian*, 1 March 1884.

who employed between 1,000 and 1,500 combers, replaced their labour with machines.[16]

While the textile industries predominated, still more than one half of the adult working population were engaged in a diversity of occupations. Within a mile or two of the town's centre were a dozen small mines, where young women and children crawed on all fours dragged loads down passages sixteen to twenty inches in height. Cheap coal, brought by canal from Wakefield, endangered the profits of local mine owners. 'The bald place upon my head is made by thrusting the corves', said Patience Kershaw of the Booth Town Pit. 'I hurry the corves a mile and more underground and back; they weigh three cwt . . . I would rather work in mill than in coal pit.' But an enlightened Board of Guardians did not allow the waifs of industrialism even this luxury of choice; in 1842 children were still 'apprenticed' at the age of eight to colliers, some of whom take 'two or three at a time, supporting themselves and their families out of their labour'. A sovereign was thrown in with each child for good measure.[17]

A small, but growing, number of the younger men found steady employment as overlookers in the mills, or in a host of textile ancillary trades, or in the iron-founding, engineering and wire-drawing concerns of the town. But the experience of many must have been similar to that of Ben Wilson, the young Chartist who lived to become the historian of the local movement:

> Tom Brown's Schooldays would have had no charm for me, as I had never been to a day school in my life; when very young I . . . was pulled out of bed between 4 and 5 o'clock to . . . take part in milking a number of cows . . . I went to a card shop afterwards, and there had to set 1,500 card teeth for a halfpenny. From 1842 to 1848 I should not

---

16. See E. Sigsworth's essay on Bradford in C. R. Fay, ed., *Round and About Industrial Britain 1830–50* (London, 1952), pp. 123–8; E. Baines, *Yorkshire Past and Present* (London, 1877), vol. 2, p. 415.

17. *First Report of the Children's Employment Commission (Mines)* (London, 1842), pp. 80, 42.

average 9/- per week wages; outdoor labour was bad to get
then and wages were very low. I have been a woollen weaver,
a comber, a navvy on the railway and a barer in the delph.[18]

Living conditions conspired with working conditions to
debase human life. The town's brook, the Hebble, was a
standing sewer; water was scarce and polluted; one twenti-
eth of the population lived in cellar dwellings. A local surgeon
William Alexander calculated that the expectation of life in
Halifax for those with money was fifty-five; for shopkeepers
twenty-four; for the working class twenty-two. The local
Bounderbys attributed the high rate of working-class mortal-
ity 'to cheap Sunday trips on the railway or to drunkenness'.
Alexander countered by drawing up solemn balance sheets
to show that improved medical services would reduce the
rates by reducing the number of pauper funerals.[19]

On all sides conditions were such to brutalize. Economic
parasitism flourished in every form: from the great
Nonconformist and Liberal mill owner at the top, Jonathan
Akroyd, through the intermediate levels of factors and
agents, beating down the weavers' wages, to the publicans
and small tradesmen who owned the 'folds', or human
warrens of damp mortar beside the Hebble, to the sub-con-
tractors in the mines and the overlookers in the mills. With
ghoulish foresight the children at the Sunday school in
Birstall were encouraged to contribute their pennies to a
burial society. The most common form of relaxation was to
be found in the beer shops, thick in the town, well scattered
on the uplands, where (in the apprehension of one anxious
local gentleman):

the incendiary and the (trade) unionist fraternize together;
from hence, under the influence and excitement of their too

---

18. B. Wilson, 'The Struggles of an Old Chartist', reprinted in D.
Vincent, *Testaments of Radicalism*, pp. 209–10.
19. W. Ranger, *Report on a Preliminary Inquiry into the Sewerage,
Drainage & Supply of Water and the Sanitary Condition of Northowram
and Southowram* (London, 1850), p. 11; Ranger, *Report . . . on the
Sewerage . . . of Halifax*, pp. 100ff.

often adulterated beverage, they turn out at midnight . . . the one to fire the corn stack and the barn, the other to imbrue his hands in the blood of a fellow workman or peradventure the man to whom he was formerly indebted for his daily bread.[20]

In the neighbourhood of the mills, infants of two and three ran around unattended, sucking rags in which were tied pieces of bread soaked in milk and water. Some of their mothers worked until the last day of pregnancy.[21]

2.

Visiting the town before the Reform Act of 1832, Cobbett had been warned by a friend that 'they were such aristocrats at Halifax, no one would come to hear me'. They did come, of course: the meeting was crowded and enthusiastic. Despite Miss Lister's belief that 'the weight of property in the borough is decidedly Conservative', the newly-enfranchised borough returned two Whigs in 1832, with a radical runner-up, and the Tory at the bottom of the poll. But Tory privilege was still a force to be reckoned with; landed families like the Listers had interests in coal, textiles, canals; the main local newspaper, the *Halifax Guardian*, was Tory; and, partly by dint of bribery and threats of eviction, the Tory candidate was assisted home against a Whig–radical coalition in 1835.[22]

If the town had its aristocratic, it also had its revolutionary traditions. Thomas Paine's *Rights of Man* had been discussed in the cottages of many weavers and combers; a local Constitutional Society had struggled against the

---

20. Crabtree, *A Concise History*, p. 18.
21. Dodd, *The Factory System*, p. 149.
22. W. Cobbett, *Report of a Lecture Speech* (Halifax, 1830); *Halifax Guardian*, 14 May 1887; J. A. Hargreaves, 'Methodism and Electoral Politics in Halifax, 1832–1848', *Northern History* 35 (1999), 139–60. 1832 results: Briggs (L), 242; Wood (L), 235; Stocks (R), 186; Wortley (C), 174; 1835: Wood (L), 336; Wortley (C), 308; Protheroe (R), 307.

forces of 'Church and King'; the reformers, never dispersed, had taken advantage of the Luddite agitation to give it – in this part of the West Riding – a revolutionary, as well as industrial, character. Cobbett's *Political Register*, T. J. Wooler's *Black Dwarf*, the unstamped press – including Joshua Hobson's *Voice of the West Riding* – circulated widely in the area, and there were men such as Robert Wilkinson ('Radical Bob'), a shoemaker, and Ben Rushton, of Ovenden, the handloom weavers' leader, whose record reached back into these years. Perhaps it was Wilkinson who was the model for a sketch by a local essayist of 'the village politician'. He was a great reader, a close student of the French Revolution and an admirer of Boney:

> It warms his old heart like a quart of mulled ale when he hears of a successful revolution, a throne tumbled, kings flying and princes scattered abroad . . . No work is done that week . . . He can tell how he was hooted, pelted and spurned . . . and people told him he might be thankful if he was not burned alive some night, along with the effigy of Tom Paine . . . He is very eloquent on the Manchester massacre and woe to the leather that is under his hammer when he is telling that tale . . . He tells queer tales about Oliver and Castle, and how one of them tried to trap him, and how it was 'no go'.[23]

Ben Rushton, the weaver, was no such comic period-piece, although he drew some of his vigour from the same radical soil. 'As steady, fearless and honest a politician as ever stood upon an English platform', he was born in 1785 and had suffered at the hands of the authorities in earlier struggles for reform. Perhaps he had known the old Paineite, John Baines, who was transported to Botany Bay for 'twisting in' Luddites. Certainly he reminds us that Luddite prisoners sang hymns on the scaffold while waiting execution; and that there were riots in Halifax when the Methodist minister refused the victims sacred burial.

---

23. E. Sloane, *Essays, Tales and Sketches* (London, 1849), pp. 61–5.

A local preacher with a wide following, it is not clear whether Rushton was formally expelled by the Methodists or whether he severed the link himself; while a Chartist leader, he was in great demand, not only at Chartist chapels and camp meetings, but also on formal occasions, such as the Sunday school anniversary in the weaving hamlet of Luddenden Dean, where he preached in worn clothing and clogs to a congregation wearing 'their best clothes, namely clogs and working clothes, including long brats or bishops'.[24]

For such men as these, agitation for radical reform passed almost imperceptibly into Chartism. The Political Unions, which organized the campaign leading to the Reform Act of 1832, remained in being. At Hebden Bridge and Todmorden (under John Fielden's leadership) these bodies supported the ten-hours agitation. It is likely that in these centres the Political Unions became, after 1832, loose popular forums from which middle-class support had been withdrawn. In Todmorden a Working Men's Association was later formed, with Fielden's support, which played an active part in the resistance to the New Poor Law before becoming identified with Chartism. In August 1839 a Todmorden magistrate was writing to the Home Office that the WMA 'has, as I conceive, been the great cause of the agitation which prevailed in this District and should if possible be broken up'.[25] In Halifax there were several years of sharp political conflict before the strands of middle-class radicalism and of Chartism were untwined. Michael Stocks, a local mine owner, who claimed to be the 'Father

---

24. *Commonwealth*, 16 November 1866; *Report of the Proceedings . . . of Oyer and Terminer . . . for the County of York* (1813), pp. 116–18; *History of Luddenden Dean Chapel* (1928), p. 5. See E. P. Thompson, *The Making*, pp. 437–40 for Rushton and 625–6, 644–5 for Baines; also J. A. Hargreaves, '"Hats Off!": Methodism and Popular Protest in the West Riding of Yorkshire in the Chartist Era: A Case Study of Benjamin Rushton', *Proceedings of the Wesley Historical Society* 57, pt. 5 (2010), 161–77 and J. A. Hargreaves, 'Benjamin Rushton, handloom weaver and radical agitator', *Oxford Dictionary of National Biography* (London, 2004).

25. H.O., 40/37. N. Pye, *The Home Office and the Chartists* (Pontypool, 2013) includes some references to the situation in Halifax.

of Reform in Halifax', fought both Whigs in 1832 on a moderate radical programme supporting the eventual implementation of household suffrage, which carried the support of influential sections of the middle class, as well as winning the applause of the hustings. During the next three years the causes of working-class discontent were multiplying. Trade unionism, widespread not only in the textile industries, but also among miners, delvers, joiners, masons and others, was met by the united resistance of the masters. The ten hours campaign heightened tension between radical mill-owners, like Jonathan Akroyd, and working people. The Tory *Halifax Guardian* was favourably disposed to factory reform (and, later, strongly anti-Poor Law), and stirred popular discontent with the Whigs skilfully.

In 1835 middle-class radicals chose as their candidate Edward Protheroe a former MP for Bristol, and formed an alliance with the Whigs (whose candidate was the sitting MP Sir Charles Wood) to fight the borough. Protheroe was a popular candidate; his defeat by one vote by the Tory led to a riot in the town. But he was in reality a political trimmer of the weakest kind, brought forward by those mill-owners like Jonathan Akroyd and his son, Edward, who were seeking a reconciliation with the 'aristocratic' Whigs. Tension still existed between the local Whig caucus and the self-made men – Nonconformists and free traders in the main – who followed the lead of Edward Baines in the *Leeds Mercury*: in February 1836 a row blew up over the appointment of magistrates, in which Whig bigwigs were denounced for constituting a 'grand, secret conclave, self-appointed, irresponsible . . . imperious and profound'.[26] But these skirmishes were little compared with the gathering resentment of rank-and-file reformers against the Whig Government and its local supporters, which first found full expression on the occasion of Feargus O'Connor's first visit to the town.

O'Connor spoke in Halifax in August 1836. He was warmly received, and a committee was formed at once

---

26. Placard 'To the Inhabitants of the Town and Parish of Halifax', 25 February 1836.

with the aim of securing his invitation to a projected dinner of the supporters of Wood and Protheroe. At least two members of the committee (Thorburn and Tetley) were later to become Chartists. The official dinner committee agreed to the proposal, but later, under pressure from the (Whig) Reform Association, rescinded the invitation. O'Connor's supporters then resolved to hold a rival dinner, declaring that 'Whiggism in Halifax is the same as Whiggism in London.'[27] Protheroe attended both dinners, but the real feast was enjoyed by the Tory *Guardian*. The Whig dinner was attended by Lord Morpeth and Edward Baines: its ceremonies were marked (to the delight of the Tories) by 'inebrity', 'bacchanalian phrensy' and 'loathsome excesses'. By contrast, the *Guardian* was pleased to note the 'moral propriety' of the radical proceedings. Of Protheroe, it aptly remarked, 'a gentleman less disposed to stand by his own opinions . . . we deny any man to find.' It is not surprising that it was O'Connor who stole the thunder. On arrival in the town he was met by 'some thousands'. In his speech he demanded manhood suffrage, lashed the New Poor Law, endorsed the ten hours movement and attacked the state church and the Ten Hours Bill. He spoke directly to the non-electors: 'You think you pay nothing? Why, it is you who pay all. It is you who pay six or eight millions of taxes for keeping up the army. For what? For keeping up the taxes.'[28]

If O'Connor fanned the storm winds, the New Poor Law was the rock on which all further hope of political unity between Akroyd's free traders and working-class reformers foundered. The struggle in the north, which opened with the visit of Assistant Commissioner Alfred Power to Huddersfield in January 1837, led directly into the Chartist alignment of forces. The attempts to enforce the New Poor Law came in a year of severe depression and bitter hardship

---

27. Leaflet 'To the Electors and Non-Electors of Halifax', 1836.
28. *Halifax Guardian*, 8 October 1836. Protheroe supported the ballot, shorter parliaments and some extension of the franchise, but not manhood suffrage: K. Rix in *The House of Commons 1832–1868* (forthcoming).

for the handloom weavers, whose independent outlook and moral sensibilities were outraged. While Huddersfield and Todmorden were the centres of outright resistance, feeling at Halifax was no less intense, though less skilfully led. A meeting of ratepayers called to nominate Guardians in February 1837 ended in disorder after a resolution denouncing the New Poor Law had been moved by Robert Wilkinson and William Thorburn. The nomination of Jonathan Akroyd was met with cries of 'The greatest tyrant in the town' and 'We want no grinders – no enemy of the Ten Hours Bill', and other radicals who supported the nomination of Guardians (on the grounds that the law of the land must be enforced) were shouted down as 'renegades'. A great public protest in March, chaired by Wilkinson, was addressed by Richard Oastler and three local preachers who were to become prominent Chartists – Ben Rushton, William Thornton and Abraham Hanson (of Elland). It is clear that the leadership of popular radicalism was now in the hands of local weavers and artisans – although, the presence of the rising carpet manufacturer Frank Crossley (whose radicalism had more in common with that of Fielden than that of Akroyd) emphasizes the fact that Halifax Chartists were always able to carry with them some middle-class support.[29]

The general election of 1837 brought a temporary revival of the old political alliance. O'Connor considered entering the contest, but in the end local radicals came in behind Protheroe. The song 'Protheroe Is the Man' was 'played by all the bands in the district and nearly every boy met whistling was almost sure to be whistling the tune'. But Protheroe's victory was little consolation.[30] The Poor Law struggle continued unabated. O'Connor addressed a meeting in August where he announced his plans for launching the *Northern Star*. The distress of the handloom weavers deepened towards

29. *Halifax Guardian*, 4 February, 1 April 1837. See Chase, *Chartism*, pp. 22–9 for the stories of Abraham and Elizabeth Hanson.

30. B. Wilson, in Vincent, *Testaments of Radicalism*, pp. 196–7. 1837 results: Protheroe (R), 496; Wood (L), 487; Wortley (C), 308.

the end of the year, and, in the Hebden Bridge district, assemblies of two or three hundred weavers waited upon the masters, demanding advances in wages.[31]

In January 1838 a meeting was held of 'Halifax radicals' which illustrates the fact that in towns such as this the various agitations which merged into Chartism were often pressed forward by the same group of reformers – whether through Political Unions, short time committees, handloom weavers' demonstrations, radical associations or other forms of organization. The chairman, William Thorburn, announced the purpose of the meeting to be the discussion of a resolution petitioning Parliament upon the five points of democratic reform. The resolution was passed, a new chairman was introduced – Ben Rushton – and the meeting went on to consider the question of the New Poor Law. Thus, some months before the People's Charter was drawn up, there existed in Halifax a vigorous local leadership, with its own organization, promoting an agitation for manhood suffrage and other radical reforms.

From this it was a short step to a meeting in July 1838 convened to establish O'Connor's recently launched Great Northern Union in Halifax. The meeting was addressed by Wilkinson, Thornton and Rushton. O'Connor spoke in extravagant style and Oastler recommended 'everyone before next Saturday night to have a brace of pistols, a good sword and a musket . . . It was the right and duty of every man to have them'. In October a Halifax contingent marched behind two bands to the first of many West Riding Chartist demonstrations at Peep Green in the Spen Valley. Wilkinson took the chair for O'Connor, Fielden, J. R. Stephens; for Peter Bussey and George White; and for Hanson and Thornton among local men.[32] By December Chartism, as an effective force, was in being. The Halifax

---

31. *Halifax Guardian*, 15 August, 28 November 1837.
32. *Halifax Guardian*, 23 January, 4 August, 20 October 1838; *Northern Star*, 4 August 1838; *Leeds Times*, 20 October 1838. The GNU was a loose and short-lived federation of radical bodies, but it, Epstein in *The Lion of Freedom*, p. 103, suggests, played a vital role in recruitment and organization in the West Riding.

magistrates applied for extra troops; but the Home Secretary could not oblige – he had 'no troops to spare'. Before the end of the year, however, a letter announced to the Halifax magistrates that a troop of the 3rd Dragoon Guards would arrive there. For the magistrates the arrival of soldiers was 'a source of great satisfaction to all respectable inhabitants and will, by the circumstances alone of it being known in the neighbourhood, give sufficient check to the ill disposed'.[33]

3.

Joseph Rayner Stephens was arrested in Ashton-under-Lyne in December 1838, and Chartist localities in all parts of the north of England held meetings of protest. In the first two weeks of January meetings were held in Halifax itself (on New Year's Day with 500 people present) and in Pellon, Mythelmroyd, Ripponden, Luddenden, Hebden Bridge and Stainland. At all of them resolutions of support for Stephens were passed, usually coupled with support for O'Connor. At Hebden Bridge the meeting affirmed the right of the people to have arms, and a week later another meeting in Halifax passed and issued to the press a strongly worded resolution which declared that 'while we are determined not to commit a breach of the peace, we are equally determined that others shall not commit a breach of the peace upon us with impunity if we can avoid it by any means in our power . . . We consider it to be both our privilege and our duty to be prepared to defend our persons and . . . our wives and families.'[34]

The West Riding delegate to the National Convention, which opened in London in February 1839, was Peter Bussey of Bradford. For many years he had been the

---

33. See G. R. Dalby, 'The Chartist Movement in Halifax and District', in *Transactions of the Halifax Antiquarian Society* (London, 1956), pp. 106–7.

34. *Northern Star*, 19 January 1839.

leading advocate of manhood suffrage in the West Riding and a man with a long record as a leader of the short-time and anti-Poor Law movements. The Halifax Chartists gave a dinner for him before he left for the Convention, where he recommended 'that every man before him should have a musket . . . and every man ought to know well the use of it'.[35] Bussey was able to take with him 52,800 signatures from his 'constituents' for the National Petition – of which 13,036 were from Halifax – and £225 National Rent – of which Halifax had collected £40 – to support the delegates. Money and signatures continued to be collected, and Halifax was represented regularly at the meetings held in the West Riding to keep in touch with their delegate. In February a town meeting called to consider Corn Law repeal was triumphantly captured by Rushton, Wilkinson and Tetley, Jonathan Akroyd and his friends retiring in discomfiture. The old radical alliance was finally shattered.[36]

Major-General Sir Charles Napier, in command of the soldiers in the Northern District, was soon to describe Halifax as 'wickedly Chartist'.[37] Even if there were more moderate counsels among the leaders, nothing could have held back the handloom weavers of the district from their preparations for insurrection. The *Guardian*, normally cautious and well informed, reported at the end of March that 700 in the neighbourhood – chiefly living in the upland hamlets – were armed with muskets. At a public house in the weaving village of Midgley firearms were being ordered.[38] In April a Halifax magistrate reported that 'there are parties . . . not only in possession of arms but undergoing drill, though then without arms in their hands . . . amongst them are many of the handloom weavers who, of all classes of work people, have experienced the greatest privations and they are prepared to amend their condition at the expense of the community when called on by their

35.   Ibid.
36.   *Halifax Guardian*, 16 February 1839.
37.   General Sir C. J. Napier, *The Life and Opinions of General Sir C. J. Napier* (London, 1857), vol. 2, p. 77.
38.   *Halifax Guardian*, 30 March 1839.

leaders'. Napier was alarmed at the scattered disposition of the cavalry in the town, and by information that there was discussion in public houses of plans to cut off the soldiers in their billets. He wrote sharply to local magistrates that 'the cavalry at Halifax are quartered in the very worst, most dangerous way ... Fifty resolute Chartists might disarm and destroy the whole in ten minutes!' Some local employers preferred the troops to remain scattered and near at hand to defend their mills. For weeks argument raged; in May, Napier wrote again 'to say I must consider the troops in that town as a force incapable of making a proper resistance in so feeble a position and therefore to be withdrawn upon the first appearance of danger'. This may have had the desired effect, for by October the magistrates were being asked to find separate accommodation for soldiers who were ill 'in consequence of the great prevalence of the Typhus fever in the town and neighbourhood and the crowded state of [the] house occupied as Barracks'.[39]

Whit Monday 1839 witnessed another great West Riding demonstration at Peep Green. Proceedings opened with a prayer, led by William Thornton: 'the sun shone on thousands of bared heads as he prayed that "the wickedness of the wicked may come to an end".' With a characteristic gesture, O'Connor clapped him on the shoulder: 'Well done, Thornton; when we get the People's Charter, I will see that you are made the Archbishop of York.' James Arran from Bradford, reported the *Guardian*, 'spoke the most rank blasphemy, said that Christ was the greatest democrat that ever lived'; Abraham Hanson denounced parsons who 'preached Christ and a crust, passive obedience and non-resistance. Let them go to those men who preached Christ and a full belly, Christ and a well-clothed back, Christ and a good house to live in, Christ and universal suffrage.'[40]

All over the country groups were discussing what

---

39.   H.O., 40/43, J. R. Ralph to Col. Wemyss, 20 April 1839; Calderdale Archives, HAS 1388/15; Dalby, 'The Chartist Movement in Halifax', pp. 108–9.

40.   Wilson, 'Struggles of an Old Chartist', in Vincent, *Testaments*, p. 198; *Halifax Guardian*, 25 May 1839. Hanson was expelled for this speech.

'ulterior measures' were to follow the rejection by the
House of Commons of the National Petition in July. There
is no doubt that some kind of armed action was considered
in Halifax. In a letter to the Home Office, the vicar of
Sowerby complained that the Chartists 'were going about
from house to house amongst the respectable shopkeepers,
inn keepers etc., threatening them if they will not support
them; one grocer, who refused his contribution, had his
name entered on a list "in red ink", as one of the first to be
attacked when they rise'.[41] The National Convention called
for a 'sacred month' or general strike to begin on 12 August.

In discussions in the Convention and throughout the
country, this proposal was coupled with the idea of an
armed rising, as violence was bound to follow such an
action. The Halifax Chartists met to consider what 'ulterior measures' they should take. One of their members,
Thomas Cliffe, had already spoken on the subject at
Bradford, where he had called for a delay in any action but
urged all Chartists to continue to procure arms. Even
speakers who urged further arming were cautious about
the strike. In the event, on the morning of Monday 12
August, between three and four hundred men assembled to
hear addresses from their leaders and to adopt an address
to the Queen. August ended with a parade through the
streets and the invasion of the parish church.[42]

For the rest of the year the public activities of the West
Riding Chartists were much diminished. The arrest of
Chartists throughout the country – though not in the West
Riding – served to intimidate some and to make others
cautious. At the same time there can be no doubt that some
secret conspiratorial organization was being built up.
William Rider, George White, Peter Bussey, 'Archbishop'
Thornton and William Cockcroft, a Halifax weaver, are
amongst those mentioned as local leaders. Frank Peel, the
historian of the Spen Valley, set down, at the end of the

41.   H.O., 40/51, letter from Revd. H. Bull, 26 July 1839.
42.   *Halifax Guardian*, 10, 17 August 1839; *Northern Star*, 17 August
1839.

century, many recollections which fill the picture of nightly drillings and secret meetings in cottages and public houses. It is likely that some time before the Newport Rising a delegate meeting was held at Heckmondwike to concert plans for a West Riding insurrection with the rest of the country.[43]

According to firm tradition, Bussey broke down and hid at the critical moment before one projected uprising. Ben Wilson, who had attended the demonstrations of 1839, although he can only have been fifteen years old at the time, says in his reminiscences that 'November . . . was fixed and Peter Bussey of Bradford was appointed leader . . . but, when the time came, Peter Bussey had fallen sick and had gone into the country out of the way or, being a shop-keeper, he was hiding in his warehouse amongst the sacks.' Wilson's view is supported by a letter sent to the Halifax magistrates by two informers: 'the Chartists . . . was casting Bullets from Saturday night until Sunday Night the Day following Joseph Spencer says he as a pike and a Gun in is possession from the information we have received had not Peter Bussey been taken badly they would of commenced the same day that Frost did' (sic). By the first week of January, Bussey was on his way to the United States, and the ballad singers in the district sang:

> I've heard Peter Bussey
> Has fledged and flown;
> Has packed up his wallet,
> And left Bradford town.[44]

---

43. F. Peel, *Spen Valley: Past and Present* (London, 1893), pp. 313ff. W. Lovett, *Life and Struggles* (London, 1967 edn.), pp. 196–9. Chase, *Chartism*, p. 109, suggests that it was a routine meeting of West Riding delegates that took place at Heckmondwike.

44. B. Wilson in Vincent, *Testaments of Radicalism*, p. 198; Dalby, 'The Chartist Movement in Halifax', p. 109. The note to the magistrates was signed by Thomas Aked and James Rawson. There was a Halifax Chartist named James Rawson. Rawson is an extremely common name in Halifax – but it is not impossible that James Rawson could have been a trusted and active Chartist and an informer. Peel, *Spen Valley*, p. 315; J. A. Hargreaves, 'Benjamin Wilson, Chartist and Horticulturist', *Oxford Dictionary of National Biography* (London, 2004).

James Stansfeld, a student with Chartist sympathies, wrote from Halifax after the Newport Rising of 3–4 November 'that secret organization was going on to a great extent I knew before as far as this neighbourhood was concerned. It was known here (among the Chartists alone, of course) when the attack was to have been made; if successful a similar movement would have been attempted here.' Reports from magistrates in Halifax give some idea of the confusion that followed the failure of the Newport Rising. A letter written a week later to the military authorities reports:

> There is a large meeting room in this town used by the Chartists . . . Last Sunday evening my informant went out of curiosity and got admittance and stayed there about three hours. Fifty persons or thereabouts were present, mostly strangers with a few townspeople . . . From the expressions of the speakers, their idea is to 'go to work' (meaning an outbreak for the purpose of plunder) and to do it in a better fashion than it had been done in Wales, where they consider it to have been sadly mismanaged. It was also said that they might as well fight 'to death' as be starved 'to death' . . . Their plan as respects this town appears to be that one of the out-townships (Ovenden, which is the worst of them) is to send its force to join friends here, and the others are to march to Bradford.[45]

Early in December James Harrison, the informer who was reporting regularly on the activities of the Bradford Chartists, told the magistrates of a visit to the Queen's Head pub near Halifax: 'One of the speakers said we have made up our minds and sent our determination down to Bradford . . . We have 260 or 270 men well armed and ammunition is ready at any time by the sound of a horn.' Harrison reported that 'the general rising is to take place . . .

---

45. J. L. and B. Hammond, *James Stansfeld* (London, 1932), p. 8. Stansfeld became Liberal MP for Halifax 1859–95, and was a close friend of Mazzini; Public Record Office, H.O., 40/43.

about the 27th . . . a place would be settled to meet the judges and to shoot them in their carriages on their way to Frost's trial.'[46]

There were no signs of any activity in Halifax or the villages around on 27 December. On the night of 11 January 1840, after the news that Frost had been found guilty, armed Chartists occupied Dewsbury, Heckmondwike and Birstall, and a special constable found the road between Bradford and Halifax 'completely filled with men, having torches and spears with them'. Later in January Bradford was the scene of an attempted rising, led by Robert Peddie, a Scot and stranger to the district. The Halifax magistrates remained worried that troops stationed in the town might be moved and the town left unprotected: 'We are still in a state of uncertainty as to whether we shall be visited by the mischievous banditti around us . . . If . . . the military force should be drawn off to a disturbance . . . they might take advantage of the opportunity and in a short time do a vast deal of damage, which now seems to be their main object'.[47]

The leaders of the Halifax Chartists were not arrested, and the local movement did not lose face as it did in Bradford and some other West Riding localities. Eighteen forty was a year of reorganization and consolidation for Chartism. The character of the movement changed dramatically after the intense excitement of the midwinter months. It was in the summer of 1840 that the National Charter Association came into existence. The Halifax branch was formed some-time during 1840, and by early 1841 Halifax and twelve branches in the out-districts made up a 'district' of the NCA. In March 1840 the Chartist meeting room, with their books, newspapers and banners, was burnt out. But meetings continued. In May James Rawson chaired a delegate meet-ing of the Halifax groups and reported that a large worsted

---

46. West Yorkshire Archives, Harewood Papers, report dated 5 December 1839; D. Thompson, *The Early Chartists* (London, 1971), pp. 280–1 for Harrison's statement in its entirety.

47. Dalby, 'The Chartist Movement in Halifax', p. 111. For Robert Peddie and the Bradford rising of January 1840 see Roberts, *Radical Politicians and Poets*, pp. 59–64.

manufacturer James Aked Junr. had reduced weavers' wages by 8–10 percent. In June a public meeting was called, protesting about the treatment of Chartist prisoners. O'Connor had proposed that money should be raised for the Chartist prisoners by adding one halfpenny to the price of the *Star*. This additional halfpenny was to be nothing to do with him, but was to be administered separately by a committee, which was to include Robert Wilkinson from Halifax. In the course of recommending the proposed increase, it was suggested that working men might find the money by buying a gill less of ale a week. Robert Sutcliffe answered this suggestion in a furious letter to the *Star*: 'Good God! To tell starving men, who cannot get a gill of ale in a month, no, nor in six months (this) . . . is a tantalising and a trifling with their poverty and misery'. Nevertheless, all through the year, Wilkinson, as treasurer, continued to send donations to the funds for prisoners' families. In June the Odd Fellows Hall was opened in Halifax, an enormous building with rooms of all sizes and a large meeting hall. After this there was no problem of a meeting place for the Chartists, however popular the speaker.[48]

The Chartists attended the hustings, at the general election in July 1841, in force, and the Liberal candidates Protheroe and Wood underwent a severe questioning from Rushton and John Crossland, a member of the handloom weavers' central committee, demanding to know why no action had been taken to relieve their plight. Wood's defence – that the only measure that would benefit the weavers was the abolition of the Corn Laws – was shouted down with cries of 'I wish thou were brought down to be a handloom weaver'. The Chartists advised support for the Tory candidate, Sir George Sinclair, a strong advocate of factory reform and an opponent of the New Poor Law. In the event, Protheroe and Wood were once again returned.[49]

---

48. *Northern Star*, 18 May, 27 June 1840; *Halifax Guardian*, 20 March, 27 June 1840.
49. *Halifax Guardian*, 12 June, 26 June, 3 July 1841. Protheroe (L), 409; Wood (L), 383; Sinclair (C), 320; Thompson, *The Chartists*, p. 273.

The work of the local association was encouraged by O'Connor's release from prison, which was announced by the Chartists through the public bellman. His visit to the town, in December 1841, was the occasion of a triumphal demonstration. A note in the *Star* described the local movement as 'progressing most gloriously . . . Numbers are coming forward to enrol their names in our association'. The work which had been put into consolidating organization brought returns when the local Chartists engaged in the collection of signatures and money for the National Petition in the early months of 1842.[50]

4

While trade was stagnant in the cotton industry, it was good and even brisk in the worsted industry in August 1842 when the Plug riots commenced. The strikers flowed through the valleys from Lancashire into Yorkshire, gathering support from the handworkers on the way. The main body of strikers crossed the Pennines from Rochdale into Todmorden on 12 August. The next day they moved up to Hebden Bridge, closing all mills, drawing the plugs from the boilers and letting off the mill dams on the way. While some of the strikers returned each night to their homes, the crowd was swelled at each stage by local workers. At Halifax 1,302 special constables were sworn in, at Hebden Bridge 170.[51]

---

50. *Northern Star*, 4 December 1841; *Halifax Guardian*, 4 December 1841. Epstein, *The Lion of Freedom*, p. 231, gives the number of NCA cards taken out in Halifax between March 1841 and October 1842 as 460. In Hebden Bridge it was 300, in Dewsbury 580 and in Bradford 1,500–1,900.

51. While some thousands of Lancashire men and women were in the West Riding, we accept the evidence of F. H. Grundy, *Pictures of the Past* (London, 1879), p. 100: 'Few people, excepting enthusiasts among the enthusiastic, marched many miles from home because multitudes were seen returning to the various towns passed through . . . I had unusual opportunities of noticing them closely and was surprised at the number whom I recognized as factory hands round about and navvies.' Also Wilson,

Contemporary accounts, as well as reminiscences, provide a vivid series of pictures of the events of the next two or three days. At dawn on 15 August an excited crowd – hearing that the approach of the strikers was imminent – assembled on Skircoat Moor. Ben Rushton addressed them, condemning the masters who had reduced wages and urging the people to support the strike and keep the peace. Upon the magistrates intervening to disperse the meeting, the crowd formed itself into a procession and marched towards Luddenden Foot to meet the Todmorden and Hebden Bridge turn-outs on their way to Halifax. Some mills were stopped on the way; the handloom weavers who joined the strike threw their shuttles into a common bag, depositing it in a public house. 'It was a remarkably fine day, the sun shone in its full splendour', one eyewitness recalled. 'The broad white road with its green hedges . . . was filled with a long, black straggling line of people, who cheerfully went along, evidently possessed of an idea that they were doing something for a betterment'. When the contingents met, 'Ben Rushton stepped aside into a field and led off with a speech . . . Before the speaking a big milk can was obtained and filled with treacle-beer. Some went into adjoining houses and were given food.'[52]

In the late morning the procession entered the town, about 5,000 strong, with women at the head, singing Chartist hymns and the One Hundreth Psalm and 'dispersed, under orders given by a man on horseback, who told them what mills to visit'.[53] Meanwhile, a formidable contingent, of between 4,000 and 5,000, were approaching the town from Bradford:

The sight was just one of those which it is impossible to forget. They came pouring down the wide road in thousands,

'Struggles of an Old Chartist', in Vincent, *Testaments*, p. 201: 'Those who attacked the soldiers at Salterhebble were neither Lancashire people nor people from a distance, but principally young men from the surrounding districts'.

52. *Halifax Guardian*, 20 August 1842; 'Memorabilia of John Hartley', *Todmorden and District News*, 1903.

53. *Illustrated London News*, 22 August 1842.

taking up its whole breadth – a gaunt, famished-looking, desperate multitude armed with huge bludgeons, flails, pitch forks and pikes, many without coats and hats, and hundreds upon hundreds with their clothes in rags and tatters. Many of the older men looked footsore and weary, but the great bulk were men in the prime of life, full of wild excitement. As they marched, they thundered out . . . a stirring melody.

Despite the efforts of the soldiers, the two contingents joined forces. The Riot Act was read, and a sharp skirmish took place between the military and the crowd before the main body dispersed – only to separate into smaller groups which closed down the remaining mills, including the largest mill of Akroyd's which the magistrates had been at great pains to defend:

> When the Riot Act was read . . . a large crowd of . . . women, who stood in front of the magistrates and the military, loudly declared that they had no homes, and dared them to kill them if they liked. They then struck up the Union Hymn:
>
>> Oh! worthy is the glorious cause,
>> Ye patriots of the union:
>> Our fathers' rights, our fathers' laws
>> Demand a faithful union.
>> A crouching dastard sure is he,
>> Who would not strive for liberty,
>> And die to make old England free
>> From all her load of tyranny,
>> Up, brave men of the union.[54]

In the skirmishes a number of prisoners were taken by the military and the special constables, and several attempts at rescue were made. Food was handed out of doors and windows to the strikers, who at length made their way to

---

54. F. Peel, *Risings of the Luddites* (London, 1880), pp. 331ff.

the moor above the town, where there were further speeches and prayers, and where a number slept in the open air.

The special constables, it seems, had drawn upon themselves both ridicule and odium during the day. They had consumed an enormous quantity of gin. Among their exploits was the capture of a sweep and the town's bellman. Their valour was displayed mainly in breaking the heads of the women. One was compared to a 'pair of tongues on horseback'. Another, to his credit, auctioned off his staff in disgust. By contrast the behaviour of the strikers was restrained, Ben Wilson recalling that 'there might have been a baker's shop or two entered, that would be the full extent'.[55]

On the next day events took a more bitter turn. The story is best told by F. H. Grundy, a civil engineer who was engaged in railway construction and had an office at Salterhebble on the Halifax–Wakefield road, just outside the town. On the morning of 16 August he found the road 'all busy, women as well as men . . . rushing along . . . with arms and aprons full of stones'. The crowd were preparing to intercept the omnibus conveying the prisoners of the previous day – with a military escort – to the railway station at Elland. The convoy passed through before their preparations were made, and the people determined to ambush the soldiers and magistrate on their return. Grundy decided to warn them, but was prevented from leaving his office by his own men. 'We two are to watch thee, like', he was informed. 'Thou'rt not to be fettled, but thou'rt to kept inside o' t'house.' At length the soldiers and the omnibus returned:

> They slow into a walk as they breast Salterhebble Hill. Then a loud voice shouts, 'Now, lads, give it 'em.' From every wall rises a crowd of infuriated men, and down comes a shower of stones, bricks, boulders . . . 'Gallop! Gallop!'

55. *The Great Plug Plot*, a scurrilous pamphlet by 'Isaac Tomkins', replied to in kind in *A Vindication of the Special Constables* (Halifax, 1842: see Dorothy Thompson Collection, Staffordshire University Library); Wilson, 'Struggles of an Old Chartist', in Vincent, *Testaments*, p. 201.

comes the order, as their leader spurs his horse up the steep hill. But the men, jammed together, cannot gallop. They come down pell-mell, horses and riders. Those who can get through ride off at speed after their officer . . . Then the command came, 'Cease throwing'. Eight horsemen, bleeding and helpless, crawled about the road . . . Down come the hosts now, and tearing the belts and accoutrements from the prostrate hussars, the saddles and bridles from the horses, they give three cheers and depart.

A report was sent express to Leeds, with an urgent demand for more troops:

A most terrible affair has occurred at Salterhebble . . . The military all out, and the special constables, too. The mob are at Skircoat Moor, and it is said here at the Northgate Hotel that they are expected down shortly when the military will, I am positively assured, receive instructions to fire . . . All the mills are closed. Mr Akroyd (I have seen him) is quite overwhelmed in difficulties. The mob keeps him at bay, and he has had his premises completely barricaded.[56]

The soldiers were not slow in taking their revenge. They sallied forth from the Northgate Inn in strength, and a good deal of indiscriminate firing took place. The main body of strikers was ridden down by the hussars, who 'followed the flying people for miles . . . Many a tale of wounded men lying out in barns and under hedges was told.' A report sent to the Home Office listed eight wounded, four dangerously. Two at least did not recover.[57]

The authorities pursued their advantage vigorously. Leading mill owners issued a notice urging all masters to re-start work, 'furnish their workmen with arms' and seize any persons found 'skulking about their premises'. By

---

56. Grundy, *Pictures of the Past*, pp. 98ff; H.O., 45/264 fos. 171–5.
57. H.O., 45/264 fos. 171–5; *Halifax Guardian*, 20 August 1842; Wilson, 'Struggles of an Old Chartist', in Vincent, *Testaments*, p. 201.

19 August many of the mills in Halifax were back at work; by 12 September the clerk to the Halifax magistrates was able to report 'business carried on as usual with the most perfect order and security'. Ben Rushton, who had been taken into custody, was released when the agitation subsided. In all thirty-six prisoners were sent to trial, and several received severe sentences – including one of transportation – for their part in the riots.[58]

5.

Halifax continued to maintain a Chartist organization in the years following the unrest of summer 1842, although in some West Riding localities organized Chartism was extinguished for several years.[59] In Halifax the organization was kept alive largely through the persistent, self-sacrificing work of local leaders. The Halifax Chartists were less troubled by quarrels and defections than most localities. They were, in general, still staunchly O'Connorite. When Bronterre O'Brien attacked O'Connor in his *National Reformer*, they took down his portrait from their walls. Ben Rushton had seen the radical cause ruined more than once by faction fights among the national leaders: he seems to have used his influence to keep the local movement free from entering too closely into national wrangles. In the mid-1840s the local leadership underwent changes. Several names pass out of the records, perhaps through death or infirmity. At least one, Thomas Cliffe, the ardent agitator of 1839, lost faith in O'Connor and left the movement. But a group of younger and equally energetic men took their places. Among them were Ben Wilson; Isaac Clissett, who

---

58. *Illustrated London News*, 22 August 1842; H.O., 45/264 fos. 171–5; E. Webster, 'Chartism in the Calder Valley, 1838–50', in *Transactions of the Halifax Antiquarian Society* (London, 1994), pp. 65–6.

59. The Chartist lecturer, John West, found Dewsbury fallen 'very low' and in Batley, with 'no person daring to let a room', there had been no meeting for some time; in Dewsbury he formed, with Rushton's help, a new association. See *Northern Star*, 10 February 1844.

had played an active part in the movement in the Spen Valley; John Snowden, a self-educated woolcomber; George Webber, a weaver; John Culpan; and Christopher Shackleton, 'the finest speaker in the district'.[60]

Chief among the local leaders, however, was still the old handloom weaver, Ben Rushton, referred to – according to preference – as 'an old bald-headed rascal' or as 'the beloved veteran in the people's cause'. His long experience, his unquestioned integrity and lack of self-interest, his 'sterling and warm-hearted good feeling' served again and again to rally the local movement. Rushton was in demand throughout the West Riding: at camp meetings, as chairman of demonstrations, and as preacher at Chartist chapels. Frank Peel has preserved an account of one such sermon, at the Chartist chapel at Littletown:

> As he depicted in glowing language, the miseries of the poor man's lot and the sin of those who lorded it so unjustly over him, the feelings of his audience were manifested by fervid ejaculations . . . until at last one, carried away by Mr Rushton's strong denunciation of oppressors, cried out, 'Ay, damn 'em, damn 'em'.[61]

The Halifax Chartists maintained their organization, and gradually extended and improved it. When the West Riding organization was revived, in February 1844, it was centred on Halifax, from where the secretaries, Crossland and later Shackleton, and the treasurer Rushton were drawn. In June 1844 the Halifax Chartists were strong enough to move into much larger rooms. The new hall was opened with lectures from George White (recently released from imprisonment and soon to settle in Bradford) and Peter Murray McDouall, the latter's quarrel with O'Connor seemingly not affecting the warmth of his reception. At these rooms

---

60. Wilson, 'Struggles of an Old Chartist', in Vincent, *Testaments*, p. 207.

61. *The Great Plug Plot*; *Northern Star*, 16 May, 8 August 1846; Peel, *Spen Valley*, pp. 317–19.

there were lectures on Sunday evenings, the meetings generally being opened by a patriotic hymn, and, for a time, classes in reading and writing. In the summer months, camp meetings, which combined the interest of a family outing and ramble with that of a political demonstration, were popular and well attended. Good relations were maintained by the local leaders with the Irish population: 'The Irish repealers . . . regularly attend Chartist meetings and in turn the Chartists do all in their power to aid and assist them.'[62]

O'Connor's Land Plan found enthusiastic support in the West Riding, and especially among handworkers. In the first year of the scheme £193 was invested by supporters in Halifax, and 'several hundred pounds' was collected at Sowerby Bridge. But, at the same time, the Land Plan gave rise to the first overt signs of dissatisfaction among Halifax Chartists with O'Connor's leadership. West Riding Chartists were disquieted by the legal side of the operation of the Land Plan. Halifax was represented at a meeting in November 1845 in the Dewsbury Co-operative Store, of Chartists from all the main West Riding centres. A number of constructive proposals were made. These were forwarded to the *Star*, but O'Connor published only a garbled version of proceedings, accompanied by an editorial attack on the organizers. The waning of O'Connor's direct influence in Halifax may perhaps be traced to these disagreements; and it is significant that, in March 1847, the town was one of only two localities in the country whose nominations for the Chartist executive did not include O'Connor's name.[63]

---

62. *Northern Star*, 13 January, 29 June, 14 September 1844. McDouall's dispute with O'Connor concerned his proposal to create a Scottish organization separate to the NCA.

63. G. J. Holyoake, *History of Co-operation in Halifax* (London, 1867), p. 16. Improvements suggested at the Dewsbury meeting included increasing the size of allotments and the prices of shares; improving the type of cottage; regularizing the position of the Land Society under the Benefit and Building Societies Act; and the appointment of independent trustees. Halifax Chartists nominated Ernest Jones, as well as John West, Daniel Donovan and David Ross (three highly regarded Irish lecturers), and Tattersall (a local man) as members of the NCA executive; the other locality which did not nominate O'Connor was Liverpool.

The years from 1843 to 1846 were ones of fair activity in the worsted and woollen industries. Unemployment diminished among the handworkers, although conditions were little changed; but improvements both in wages and conditions were marked within the walls of the mills.[64] In 1846, when the ten-hours agitation revived, a leading part was taken by local Chartists, among them the handloom weavers who hoped that a limitation in the hours worked in the factories would increase the demand for their labour. Some slight connections had been built up between some Chartists and some leading Liberals in the town through the formation of the Halifax Union Building Society, which aimed to secure the purchase by working men of votes by means of acquiring 40/- freeholdings in county constituencies. This time it was the ten-hours agitation upon which this tentative alliance foundered, the prominent Liberal, young Edward Akroyd, incurring odium by the vigour with which he led the resistance to the ten hours bill. The once-radical Protheroe brought the Liberal cause into deeper discredit by becoming involved in a personal scandal. When Rushton, in November 1846, took the chair for Oastler and Fielden, he was riding the incoming tide of renewed Chartist popularity.[65]

Meanwhile, a new star had risen on the Halifax horizon. In August 1846 there had taken place one of those striking demonstrations when the Chartists of Lancashire and Yorkshire joined forces on the high and remote moor of Blackstone Edge. Many thousands were present and Rushton

---

64. *Halifax Guardian*, 11 July 1846, for a report by one working man that, some years before, one of his daughters was paid one shilling a week for working about fourteen hours a day at Akroyd's mill, but her younger sister was now paid 2s 6d a week for working about six hours a day.

65. *Halifax Guardian*, 12 September, 14 November 1846; E. Akroyd, *On Improved Dwellings for the Working Classes* (London, 1846); J. L. and B. Hammond, *James Stansfield*, p. 15. Protheroe was accused by his valet of homosexual practices, and the matter was made a great deal worse by the savage sentence of twenty years transportation imposed on the valet for attempted blackmail (*Halifax Guardian*, 31 October 1846). This was not to be the last time Protheroe was involved in legal proceedings in regard to his alleged homosexuality.

took the chair. He then called on 'Ernest Jones, Esq., barrister-at-law, who would make his maiden speech to his new allies.'[66]

6.

Ernest Jones was convinced that the heart of the Chartist movement lay in the industrial north. He attended the Leeds Convention of August 1846 as delegate for the Limehouse Chartists, but later the same year was asked to stand for election as a full-time officer in London. This offer was apparently turned down. He was later to turn down another offer, this time from the Edinburgh Chartists to undertake the editorship of the *North British Express*, for which they would 'allow a liberal salary, the amount of which they leave to yourself'. Both these offers would have given Jones a position and an income at a time when he had very few private resources; but it seems clear that he was not prepared to take work which would take him away from the West Riding.

Jones's association with Halifax was cemented by the election campaign in 1847.[67] Sir Charles Wood, the Liberal MP for the constituency and a member of the Government, had lost much support because of his association with a bill for state-aided education, a measure against which Nonconformists throughout the country were up in arms. The Halifax Nonconformists turned to Edward Miall, the editor of the *Nonconformist*, and his willingness to associate with Jones robbed Protheroe of what stomach he had for the fight. Protheroe retired from the contest shortly

---

66. *Northern Star*, 8 August 1846.
67. Columbia University Library, Seligman Collection, J. Grant to E. Jones, 24 May 1848. The Leeds conference was notable for Jones moving a motion for the expulsion of Thomas Cooper: see Roberts, *The Chartist Prisoners*, pp. 90–1. The 1847 Halifax election is discussed in K. Tiller, 'Late Chartism: Halifax 1847–58', in J. Epstein and D. Thompson, eds, *The Chartist Experience* (London, 1982), pp. 314–15; J. A. Jowitt, 'A Crossroads in Halifax Politics: The Election of 1847', *Transactions of the Halifax Antiquarian Society* (1973–74), pp. 19–36.

before nomination day – an event which greatly encouraged Chartist hopes. Henry Edwards seems to have been a typical Halifax Tory: a local landowner and employer, a firm opponent of free trade but a supporter of the ten hours bill – whose provisions he enforced in his own works sometimes before its parliamentary enactment – and an opponent of the New Poor Law. His limited powers of oratory made him something of a joke during the election. Miall and Jones were close in their immediate programme, but in many ways their policies were very different. Miall, already known as an advocate of manhood suffrage, was prepared to accept other Chartist points, but his main concern was the separation of Church and State, particularly with regard to education. If the principles of the Charter were secondary questions for Miall, there is no doubt that the religious and educational questions came a very poor second for the majority of Chartists, including their candidate.[68]

Jones won the loyalty of the local movement to an extraordinary degree; and this, combined with the dissension in the opposition and the coincidence of a trade recession in the woollen and worsted industries which began in the summer of 1847, resulted in an atmosphere of enthusiasm and excitement which had not characterized the activities of local Chartists for several years. Jones was an excellent candidate. Ben Wilson recalled that 'nearly everybody seemed to know him as he walked through the streets. He had a noble and striking appearance.' All the local stalwarts threw their efforts into the election campaign. They sought out and publicized the names of tradesmen sympathetic to their cause and called on all Chartist supporters – whether electors or not – to patronize only these shops. The *Guardian* attacked this policy of 'exclusive dealing', and the Whigs placarded the town in protest. Despite such protests (which were testimony to the effectiveness of the system), the Chartists intensified the pressure, even dividing the town into wards in which favoured

---

68. *Northern Star*, 24 July 1847. M. Taylor, *Ernest Jones, Chartism and the Romance of Politics, 1819–1869* (Oxford, 2003), p. 103, notes that Jones and Miall had little contact during the campaign.

shopkeepers were recommended. Ben Wilson described how large numbers of working people visited the shops of supporters of Jones and collected outside the shops of supporters of Wood and Edwards and hooted their customers. 'Mr Boddy, a grocer in Northgate', he recalled, 'did a large amount of business for many years and then retired. He erected the fine body of buildings in Northgate known as "Boddy's Building" and it was said that he saved the bulk of the money out of the profits of that agitation.' But the main form of electioneering was the organization of meetings and counter-meetings, demonstrations and counter-demonstrations. On 11 July the Chartists attended a camp meeting on Blackstone Edge, attended by thousands from Yorkshire and Lancashire. The following week Jones reported to the *Star* a meeting at which he addressed 10,000 from a window at the Bull's Head. In the face of the Chartist opposition, Wood and Edwards came gradually closer together; the voting results clearly show a coalition against Chartism and Dissent between the supporters of the two candidates, although this was at the time officially denied by the Whigs.[69]

As nomination day drew near, the excitement increased. Placards were issued announcing a public meeting at the Northgate Hotel, to hear Wood, 'The awful events of that evening', wrote the *Guardian*, 'will cause the borough election of 1847 long to be remembered in the history of Halifax'. At the outset the meeting room was invaded by working people. 'The room was in a very few moments nearly filled, chiefly with non-electors', the report continues. 'We observed several of the leading friends of Miall and Jones in the body of the meeting.' The meeting was opened by the chairman, Jonathan Akroyd, who began by trying to justify the proposed education scheme, but was interrupted to such an extent that at one time he was forced to stop whilst order was restored. When he continued, he managed only a few words 'and then, as if making a bow to the meeting, he fell forward upon the

69. *Halifax Courier*, 31 January 1891; *Halifax Guardian*, 10 July, 17 July 1847; *Northern Star*, 17 July 1847; Wilson, 'Struggles of an Old Chartist', in Vincent, *Testaments*, p. 205.

table – dead . . . it is needless to say that every gentleman present was convulsed with grief.' The inquest of Jonathan Akroyd returned a verdict of 'Death by the visitation of God'. He was buried at Salem Chapel, but was subsequently converted to Anglicanism by his son, Edward, who – in 1856 – dug up the remains of his parents and had them re-interred in his own Church of All Souls at Haley Hill. So the pre-election speech of Sir Charles Wood was never delivered, and it may well be that the sentiments aroused amongst Liberals in the town by the pathetic circumstances of the death of Akroyd did more for his chances than the speech would have done.[70]

Nomination day was a day of suppressed excitement. The authorities were clearly apprehensive of trouble, and a troop of cavalry was stationed in the town; but, at the hustings, there was no worse disorder than shouting and interjections. The greatest applause of the 10–11,000 spectators was reserved for Jones. At the show of hands not more than a hundred voted for Wood; for Edwards between 2,000–3,000, whilst for Jones and Miall about 7,000 hands were raised. Jones and Miall were declared elected, and a poll was demanded on behalf of Wood and Edwards. After such a triumph at the hustings, the Chartists were bitterly disappointed at the results of the poll. Wood and Evans were returned with 507 and 511; Miall polled 351 and Jones 280. In spite of their defeat the Chartists celebrated handsomely: two weeks later thousands turned out, some 1,200 ticket holders to join events within the hall, and the rest to wait outside – to be addressed by Jones in the intervals between sittings. The hall was decorated with banners, slogans and portraits of Chartist and radical leaders. The women, determined that the radical colour should be well represented, turned up with green ribbons in their caps, green handkerchiefs and some even in green dresses. When Jones rose to speak, the people cheered for several minutes.[71]

---

70. *Halifax Guardian*, 31 July 1847.
71. *Halifax Guardian*, 31 July, 28 August 1847.

Trade was declining in the later months of the year, but, despite unemployment and distress, the Halifax Chartists kept their organization going, meeting regularly on Saturday evenings and also sending representatives to the periodic West Riding delegate meetings. In August 1847 a meeting of 2,000 female Chartists agreed to carry on exclusive dealing. At the opening of 1848 the *Guardian* gave the number of destitute unemployed in Halifax as 1,577, chiefly among weavers and combers at Ovenden. This figure took no account of short time in the mills or of partial unemployment among weavers; and the inadequate weekly expenditure of £100 by the relief committee must have left many in the town faced with actual starvation. Voluntary subscriptions were raised and some relief work started on roads and on the new reservoir, with payment at the rate of 2d an hour and a maximum of six hours a day. The relief committee kept a sharp check on all men so employed, visiting their homes to make sure that they were destitute and enforcing a rigorous punctuality. In February 1848 a demonstration of 400 woolcombers from Ovenden marched to the workhouse, demanding not relief but employment. At their approach the gates were hurriedly barred, but a deputation of eight was finally admitted. These eight leaders were offered relief, but they refused until their comrades were relieved also. These were times, as Ben Wilson said, that 'made politicians'.[72]

7.

Although Chartist activity in the West Riding, as in other parts of England, was already greater in the winter of 1847–48 than it had been for some years, there is no doubt that it was greatly stimulated by events in France. Following the French Revolution of February 1848, some members of

---

72. *Northern Star*, 14 August 1847; *Halifax Guardian*, 8 January, 15 January 1848; 'Halifax in the Forties', in *Courier and Guardian Almanack*, 1901; Wilson, 'Struggles of an Old Chartist', in Vincent, *Testaments*, p. 206.

the movement may have contemplated a direct confrontation with the armed forces of the Crown, but a far greater number, which included O'Connor and the other national leaders, believed that a demonstration of force would be sufficient to coerce the government. In Halifax many new recruits joined the Chartists, particularly from among the younger people. It was at this time that Ben Wilson reported working men marching through the streets in military order. The slogan 'France has the Republic, England shall have the Charter' accompanied this drilling.

The first reaction to events in France was a meeting at the Odd Fellows Hall to welcome the revolution. The meeting was chaired by Jonathan Gaukroger, who introduced it with an appeal to the principles of moral force. This, the *Guardian* reported, was booed in places by 'the younger element'. Resolutions, introduced by Isaac Clisset and James Boden, congratulated the French and called for the implementation of the People's Charter. At another meeting, in April, Jones was unanimously elected to represent Halifax at the forthcoming National Convention. Marching back from the rally, the Chartists passed the barracks, where they were cheered by the soldiers. Such conduct so alarmed the authorities that within a few days the soldiers were ordered to be transferred to Dublin. On the day of their departure, 5,000 Chartists turned out, with tricolour flags and a brass band to accompany them to the railway station.[73]

Tension rose throughout April. The collection of signatures for the National Petition embraced wide sections of the population: a Baptist minister at Queenshead concluded his sermon by explaining the points of the Charter and laying the petition for signature on the vestry table. There were repeated outdoor meetings. Open drilling took place; arming was widespread. Ben Wilson recalls how he was drawn into this side of things: 'I . . . purchased a gun, although I knew it was a serious thing for a Chartist to have a gun or pike in his possession . . . I well remember

---

73. *Halifax Guardian*, 18 March 1848; D. Thompson, *The Chartists*, p. 312.

only a few years ago some talk with a friend who told me he was moulding bullets in his cellar in 1848'. Jones, speaking on behalf of his 'constituents' at the National Convention, described their mood: 'they warned him not to stoop to one act of unnecessary humility in urging their claims. To a man they were ready to fight', Jones told the National Convention of the Halifax Chartists.[74]

The Halifax magistrates prepared for trouble. On one day 500 special constables were sworn in. In the event they were not given the opportunity to show whether they were made of better material than their predecessors of 1842. At least one special constable's stave appeared in the hands of a speaker on a Chartist platform, garlanded with a tricoloured ribbon. The order from London banning the Kennington Common meeting was printed in full in Halifax, with a further warning from local magistrates cautioning the curious from mixing with dangerous men. In spite of the warnings, however, thousands attended a camp meeting on Skircoat Moor on 10 April and afterwards marched to the town centre where George Webber addressed them from a window of Nicholl's Temperance Hotel. Rumours circulated freely, including one that Jones had been shot. Webber declared to the crowd that he 'had no doubt that, if a drop of Ernest Jones's blood were spilt, the men of Halifax would avenge it. (Great applause and shouts of "We will!")'.[75]

In London itself the events of 10 April appeared as an anti-climax. The *Guardian* sounded a note, not of victory, but of extreme alarm, devoting no less than three editorials to admonishing the working man and going even to the extreme (for an Anglican and Tory newspaper) of quoting Pope Pius IX, no doubt for the enlightenment of the Irish labourers. On Good Friday a crowd of 20,000 assembled on Skircoat Moor. The procession through the town was

---

74. Wilson, 'Struggles of an Old Chartist', in Vincent, *Testaments*, p. 209; *Northern Star*, 8 April 1848.

75. *Halifax Guardian*, 8 April, 15 April 1848. See *Halifax Courier*, 16 February 1895, for obituary for Webber.

itself more than 10,000 strong, accompanied by twelve bands and a sea of banners. The banners were menacing in tone, declaring 'We conquer or die' and 'Tyrants, prepare to meet your God'. Women marched prominently in the procession, bearing such legends as 'Mothers, claim the rights of your children'. The speakers were the local men, as the national figures were still occupied with the Convention in London. The former Methodist preacher Joseph Barker recorded that he found himself very isolated after the expression of his views on the necessity of moral force only. But the meeting, for all the great numbers, passed off completely peacefully. Magistrates testified to the zeal and good conduct of the Second West Yorkshire Cavalry on the occasion.[76]

The National Convention dissolved, with no formal decisions taken, in May. The comparatively high level of organization in Halifax was evident in the fact that local Chartists contributed £10 to the expenses of the Convention – by far the largest donation reported in the *Star*. The leadership of the active portion of the movement fell more and more into Jones's hands. In a letter addressed to 'The Men of Halifax', his main call was for improved organization, preparation and agitation. The Halifax Chartists obeyed Jones's call. Undeterred by their defeat in the parliamentary election of the year before, the Chartists organized to return their chosen candidates in the first municipal elections in the town, once again in alliance with radical Dissent. According to Ben Wilson, the friends of Jones and Miall carried all before them and three members of the Ackroyd family were defeated. A black flag was hoisted in triumph from Nicholl's Temperance Hotel. The effect of Chartist support for the radical candidates seems to have been a drawing together of some of the more radical middle-class politicians with the Chartists. The first town meeting soon after the elections passed a series of resolutions directly relating to the demands of the Chartists. They were moved

---

76. *Halifax Guardian*, 15 April, 21 April 1848. For Barker see S. Roberts, 'Joseph Barker and the Radical Cause, 1848–51', *Publications of the Thoresby Society* (1990), pp. 59–73.

by the radicals, seconded by the Chartists and signed by the mayor, who sent them to Sir Charles Wood.[77]

After the confusion of the National Convention and the rejection of the National Petition, many people began to celebrate the demise of Chartism. When Richard Cobden declared the Chartists to be 'a small, insignificant and power-less party', the *Guardian* took him to task: 'There are a few people in Lancashire and Yorkshire who can tell him a different story . . . We have no wish to overrate the numbers or import of the Chartist body, but men who muster in tens of thousands to demonstrate their attachment to a political principle are neither "small" nor "insignificant".' The Home Secretary began to advise magistrates to take action against drilling: in Bradford and Bingley arrests were made but, in Halifax, the magistrates held their hand.[78]

A camp meeting was arranged to take place on Blackstone Edge on 11 June at which Jones was to be one of the main speakers; but a Manchester Chartist arrived with the news that he had been arrested. The Young Ireland trials, with their sentences of transportation, were fresh in the minds of the Halifax Chartists, and they formed a procession and marched on to the moors. Webber addressed them by torch-light, declaring 'that if a similar sentence should be passed on Jones . . . they would erect barricades . . . and, if necessary, proclaim the republic of Yorkshire and Lancashire'. The authorities were careful, when choosing which of the Chartist leaders to arrest in 1848, to concentrate on those who had influence in the north – in addition to Jones, McDouall, White and West were arrested, all men who had a consider-able following in Halifax. Later some local men were arrested for drilling or seditious speeches, amongst whom were Webber, who served a sentence for sedition, and Joseph

77. *Northern Star*, 20 May 1848; *Halifax Reformer*, 24 May 1848; *Halifax Courier*, 16 November, 23 November 1901; Tiller, 'Late Chartism', in Epstein and Thompson, *The Chartist Experience*, pp. 316–17. Webster, in 'Chartism in the Calder Valley', p. 71, doubts – probably correctly – that the four men described as Chartist councillors (a property owner, an innkeeper, a corn dealer and a linen draper) were actually Chartists.

78. *Halifax Guardian*, 27 May 1848.

Lemming, who was sentenced for drilling. It seems that the other local leaders were not imprisoned that summer: certainly none of the well-known Halifax names appears in the lists of trials at York, Manchester or Liverpool. The *Guardian* welcomed the arrest of Jones and began to show signs of being extremely worried by the continued mood of excitement in the district. It reported that on one night in August 'hundreds of men sat up with pikes in hand, ready to fight' but that the pre-arranged signal did not come. However, Ben Wilson, although he took part in the 'physical force' side of the movement, makes no mention of any such plan.[79]

The trial of Jones for sedition in July 1848 was closely followed by the Halifax men, some of whom travelled to London to arrange bail. Jones was sentenced to two years' imprisonment, and soon after the West Riding delegate meeting passed a strongly-worded resolution which declared that the Chartist campaign had failed 'in consequence of being based on moral arguments in opposition to an authority based on physical power and . . . that no other means short of that by which the people are opposed will ever gain their rights and privileges'. But if this resolution represented a new turn towards a determined insurrectionary strategy, the moment for that strategy to be employed with any hope of success had already gone by. Nor was the moment to return.[80]

8.

There were a number of reasons for the change in political climate – and for the failure of the preparations of such men as Webber to lead to any effective conclusion. In the first place, it seems clear that the spirit manifested in the

79. *Halifax Guardian*, 17 June, 19 August 1848. The *Guardian* (27 May 1848) was concerned to the extent of blossoming forth into a verse in an effort to appeal to the better natures of working men: 'Remember you are Englishmen and up and proudly tell/The traitors that would tempt you or would teach you to rebel/We're poor but we are loyal men, we'll be as we have been/True to ourselves, our honest hearts, our country and our Queen'.

80. *Northern Star*, 22 July 1848.

West Riding was, by the end of July, confined almost entirely to the West Riding and to parts of Lancashire. The national leadership, as exemplified by the *Star*, was certainly not of an insurrectionary character. Jones, in his last letters and speeches before imprisonment, had urged the need for organization; but the other leaders seemed more concerned with recriminations for past errors than the reorganization of the movement. But perhaps more significant in changing the atmosphere, and certainly more important in its long-term implications, was the sudden and very considerable improvement which took place in the later months of 1848 in both the woollen and worsted industries. While in the worsted industry most hand weaving had by now been replaced by power, the upward turn in trade brought a respite of several years to the hand combers in the Halifax district. In the woollen industry, where hand weaving was still very widely employed, the improvement in trade was a few months delayed: but 1849 was to see an increase of nearly 60 per cent in the export of woollen pieces over 1848. For many years in the upper Calder Valley and Huddersfield districts the old 'poverty-knockers' were still to ply their trade.

And yet it is reasonable to assume that the centre of gravity of working-class political agitation was now passing away from the handworkers into the mills and factories of the booming industrial centres. The twenty-year agony of the weavers had decimated their ranks. Young working men now sought employment in towns or along the railways; other emigrated. Those who were too old, or who clung to their occupations and communities, tended to cling also to an outlook which was becoming foreign to their sons and brothers in the factory towns, who were coming to accept the industrial system in a way in which their forefathers who eagerly read Cobbett and followed Oastler could not do. The turbulent demonstrations of March to August 1848 in the Halifax and Bradford areas can be seen as closely related to the last desperate protest of the handworkers. Certainly the agitation was by no means confined to these workers alone; but the outlook of these workers, their hatred of the factory system, their nostalgic yearning for land and economic independence, their combination of ineffective industrial organization with extreme political radicalism, was likely to divide them from the main currents of opinion among the younger factory workers in the industrial towns. There is no evidence that these divisions in outlook led to any sharp conflict among the core of the Halifax Chartists, who were held together by common political conviction and loyalty. But there is evidence enough that the Chartist agitators met with gathering defeatism and apathy among the people; and evidence also that the local mill owners turned their attention, after the mid-1840s, with greater subtlety, determination and effect to the task of winning over the minds of the working class.

In the West Riding boom conditions in the worsted industry lasted throughout 1849 and 1850. Halifax maintained its place second to Bradford in the industry, with seventy-five firms employing 16,601 workers. Many new mills were built: December 1849 saw the opening of Akroyd's great new Bowling Dyke mills with a grand celebration concert, including *The Creation* by Haydn, attended by 2,000 workers. Despite a certain falling-away in trade in 1851, the general expansion continued. The solution of the problem of the application of power-loom weaving to carpets led to the great expansion of Crossley's mills at Dean Clough in 1852, where 'weavers were working day and night . . . and new power looms sprung up like mushrooms.' In such an economic climate it became possible for free-trade politicians to gain the ear of the working man and for schemes of working-class self-help to be carried out. Libraries in chapels and improvement societies in the Halifax district are testimony to the energy with which the clergy and lay missionaries sought to bring the Light from Manchester into Darkest Proletaria more than a decade before Samuel Smiles's *Self-Help* appeared. Edward Akroyd (the son of Jonathan), with the building of the model village at Copley, embarked on a career of paternalism that was to lead him to promote building societies, a horticultural society, allotments, clothing clubs, a working man's college, young women's institutes and a penny bank.[81]

Within this new context, it is surprising, not that there was something of a rapprochement between the Halifax Chartists and the middle-class radicals, nor that there were developments of new forms of activity (notably co-operation), but that the local movement remained so steadfast in maintaining both the principles and organization of Chartism. This may be attributed in part to the strength of mind of leaders such as Ben Rushton; in part to the direct influence of Ernest Jones. But at the same time it is important not to exaggerate the degree of alteration in the social climate in the boom years after 1848. The general extreme misery of the mass of the workers was little alleviated in the 1850s. Thomas Latimer, who took part in establishing the Liberal *Halifax Courier*, recalled the atmosphere of the town in 1854: 'I found . . . a bitterness of spirit dividing the capitalist and the workman which was very painful to witness – the separation was so sharply defined.'[82]

9.

Throughout Ernest Jones's imprisonment, the Halifax Chartists made regular collections of money for his wife and children. In December 1848 there was a parliamentary by-election in the West Riding which the Chartists decided to contest. Samuel Kydd, one of the most influential of the unimprisoned Chartist leaders and a member of the NCA executive, appeared as the candidate, and each of the Chartist localities in West Riding was asked to attend the hustings at Wakefield, bringing an elector in their party. The Halifax contingent took with them Joseph Hanson of the famous Crispin Inn. Kydd received the overwhelming majority in the show of hands, but did not go to the poll. After the meeting some of the Halifax men walked to

81.   *Halifax Courier*, 7 July 1888.
82.   F. R. Spark, *Memories of My Life* (London, 1913), pp. 88–9.

Batley, where O'Connor was paying one of his now rare visits to the district. He spoke to a packed room and 'quite electrified the audience'. This was among his last visits to the West Riding.[83]

The main burden of work now fell to the small band of convinced Chartists. Many of these were young men in their twenties. The secretary of the locality was John Culpan, a talented debater and writer. But popular support for Chartism was on the decline. National figures such as Kydd and R. G. Gammage were still engaged to give lectures, but 'it appeared to be to no purpose for very few came to hear them'. With the improvement in trade and the falling off of other forms of activity, there was a general turn among many Chartists towards consumer's co-operation. Support for co-operative principles had always been strong in the West Riding, though stronger in Huddersfield and on the Lancashire border than in Halifax itself. In Hebden Bridge the founders of what was to become one of the most vigorous co-operative centres in the north were Chartists. In Halifax in January 1849 placards were issued announcing the first meeting of the Co-operative Trading Society, but it lasted for five months only and the small trading capital which its original members had contributed was lost. But the Chartists did not give up at this. Indeed, although the Halifax Industrial Society dates its existence officially from 1851, more than one false start was made. When firmly established, Chartists were still to the fore, and such men as Wilson and Webber served as directors throughout the fifties and sixties. [84]

A stimulus was given to the movement by the release from prison of Ernest Jones in July 1850. He was given a tumultuous welcome in Halifax, one of the first places he visited. A great demonstration met him and Julian Harney

83. Wilson, 'Struggles of an Old Chartist', Vincent, *Testaments,* p. 211. The Crispin Inn had long associations with Halifax radicalism – the Luddites, for example, had used it as a meeting place.

84. Wilson, 'Struggles of an Old Chartist', in Vincent, *Testaments*, p. 213. R. Blatchford, *History of the Halifax Industrial Society* (Halifax, 1901).

at the railway station, and in an open carriage drawn by four greys and with a band of music, the two men proceeded to a gala in West Hill Park. At the meeting a purse of thirty-eight guineas was presented to Jones, and Ben Wilson recalled that, at the reception that evening at Nicholl's Hotel, he refused an invitation from a group of middle-class gentlemen to attend a private meeting and instead spent his time amongst the Chartists. The following evening the Chartist committee, thirty or so in number, entertained Jones and Harney to dinner and a 'jovial evening'.[85]

The loyalty of the Halifax Chartists touched Jones deeply. His poem 'Beldagon Church', which appeared in May 1851, was prefaced with a long dedication to them. He was appointed their delegate to the Chartist Convention that year in London, but the quarrels and defections among the national leadership, which culminated in a breach between Jones and Harney and the Manchester Convention of 1852, were not without effect in the district. Halifax (represented by William Cockcroft) was one of the handful of localities represented at the Convention, and gave its support to the new executive of three. But Harney's supporters included Christopher Shackleton and George White, and there was a period of fierce dissension among the West Riding Chartists before the issue was resolved in Jones's favour 'and many who had been very strongly opposed to him became his friends'. 'I have often thought', wrote Wilson, with an understatement which throws these years of rank-and-file devotion into sharp relief, 'that, if the leaders of our movement could have worked a little more harmoniously together at times, we might have been more powerful.' On the formation of the *People's Paper* in May 1852, Wilson wrote to Jones asking him to keep personal quarrels out of the paper. 'Not one syllable of personality shall intrude itself into its columns', was Jones's response.

---

85. *Halifax Guardian*, 20 July 1850; *Northern Star*, 20 July 1850; Wilson, 'Struggles of an Old Chartist', in Vincent, *Testaments*, p. 214. The Thompsons also refer intriguingly at this point to J. Ramsden, MS Notebook 'in our possession'; this volume is not in Calderdale Archives and its whereabouts are unknown.

Throughout its existence, Halifax Chartists raised weekly contributions to help keep the newspaper going.[86]

In the winter of 1851–52 the woolcombers of the district struck against repeated wage reductions – a prelude to their complete replacement by machinery in the next three or four years. Jones encouraged them in print. In July 1852 he again contested Halifax as a Chartist candidate. The atmosphere was by no means as tense as in 1847, although on the night of the election there were plenty of incidents, including the 'bottling' of Chartist voters and their forcible rescue. According to Gammage (a witness unlikely to show undue favour to him), Jones delivered 'one of the most powerful and magnificent orations ever listened to'. Jones overwhelmingly won the show of hands; but the official poll the next day showed a great falling-off in support – Jones gained only thirty-seven votes. When a by-election followed soon afterwards, the Chartists determined not to contest again, but demonstrated their neutrality on the day of the poll by gathering their sympathizers among the electors into an upstairs room in Nicholl's Hotel and guarding the stairway against the forcible intrusion of canvassers.[87]

The funeral of Ben Rushton on 26 June 1853 was the last great West Riding demonstration. Jones hailed the occasion optimistically as a revival of Chartism, but, though it was indeed an event of importance, he mistook the tribute to the man who represented in his own person the dignity of the Chartist prime for evidence of a new determination. The coffin, carried by six of the oldest Chartists in the town, was followed by a procession many thousands strong. Five extra trains brought people from Bradford,

---

86. E. Jones, *Notes to the People*, vol. 1 (London, 1851), pp. 21–7; Wilson, 'Struggles of an Old Chartist', in Vincent, *Testaments*, pp. 215–16. Halifax Chartists sent £30 to support the *People's Paper* in the first three months of its existence.

87. Gammage, *History of the Chartist Movement*, p. 391; Tiller, 'Late Chartism', in Epstein and D. Thompson, *The Chartist Experience*, pp. 322–5. The complaint about the 'bottling' of Chartist electors originated with Jones.

whilst another contingent, with a band, marched over the hills by road. Rushton had expressed the wish that no paid priest officiate at his burial, and the orations were given by Jones and Gammage, with the final words pronounced by another Halifax veteran, Robert Sutcliffe. After the ceremony the procession walked the two miles back to the town, and a meeting in favour of the People's Charter was held.[88]

The Halifax Chartists continued to organize lectures for several more years, paying about ten shillings (which included expenses) to secure speakers like Harney and Kydd. In 1857 John Frost, pardoned at last, came to the town and lectured on penal reform. The Chartists welcomed him warmly, for his release had been an important part of their programme since 1840. The local Chartist association was still in existence in December 1857 and appointed John Snowden as their delegate to the Chartist Convention of February 1858. The *People's Paper* had continued to circulate in the district, and its demise in September 1858 was a serious blow. The agitation for the People's Charter had now come to an end. In autumn 1859 Jones was in an even worse financial situation than usual and wrote to former supporters appealing for help. 'I am sorry to inform you that there is no Chartist organization in Halifax nor any of the numerous villages surrounding it', John Snowden replied, adding that 'once active Chartists have emigrated and others . . . so thoroughly disgusted at the indifference and utter inattention of the multitude . . . are resolved to make no more sacrifices in a public cause'.[89]

Snowden was not – in 1859 – an entirely reliable witness. Reduced to the workhouse his Chartist friends collected money for him, but he refused their assistance. Later, however, he accepted a pension of ten shillings a week from

88. *People's Paper*, 2 July 1853; *Halifax Evening Courier*, 24 June 1976.

89. *People's Paper*, 14 April 1855, 7 June 1856; J. Snowden to E. Jones, 16 October 1859, Chetham's Library, Manchester; See Tiller, 'Late Chartism', in Epstein and D. Thompson, *The Chartist Experience*, pp. 327–35, for a much fuller picture of events in the mid-to-late 1850s.

Edward Akroyd, on whose election committee he served in 1868. A pamphlet from his hand *Radicalism Vindicated* (1867) reveals a self-educated mind cluttered with the antiquities and precedents of democracy, contemptuous of fellow workers who had failed to attain the same knowledge as himself. He allowed himself to be used, on platforms as far afield as Manchester, as a specimen of the sober working man who had no truck with the excesses of the Reform League. At the same time, a small group of Chartists, including Wilson and Webber, continued to meet who did not share Snowden's pessimism and who regarded their old friend as a defaulter.

There certainly existed in Halifax a direct, if tenuous, organizational link between Chartism and the Reform League, and a section of opinion in the town regarded itself as distinct from middle-class radicalism. Webber was the moving spirit, and secretary, of the Halifax branch of the Reform League. The Chartist survivors, like Wilson, were at his side. At Rippenden Samuel Moores pressed forward the agitation. In September 1866 the Odd Fellows Hall was packed to capacity, with hundreds unable to gain entrance, when once again Ernest Jones – supported by Edmund Beales, George Potter and Webber – addressed a great meeting calling for manhood suffrage. In the general election of 1868 Chartists and radicals united in a last agitation before merging into the stream of Gladstonian Liberalism.[90]

Edward Akroyd was now a Liberal MP for Halifax, and this autocratic industrial grandee, with his extravagant paternalism and long enmity towards the Chartists, soon alienated radical opinion. Webber and the Reform League initiated a committee to bring forward a radical candidate to oust him. Their first choice was Jones, but he was already committed to Manchester. On his advice they selected Edward Owen Greening, a rising man in the co-operative movement, and a sharp contest took place in November 1868. Jones and his wife were invited as guests of honour to the tea meeting to celebrate the campaign. Jones's funeral

---

90. *Halifax Guardian*, 8 September 1866.

in the same month (January 1869) was attended by four delegates from the Halifax Reform League, including Webber and Wilson.[91]

Thereafter there were tributes to veterans and reminiscent meetings enough. Snowden joined his old friends in raising money for Jones's widow. Later Hebden Bridge Chartists were prominent in raising the memorial to Jones in Ardwick. In 1885 Ben Wilson called together a meeting at Maude's Temperance Hotel of old Chartist friends: Culpan, Shackleton and Webber and nearly twenty others were present. The best thanks of the meeting were given to Gladstone and to the Liberal MPs for various blessings. No one thanked the old Chartists, but the local newspapers took some notice of this political curiosity: 'the majority of those attending the meeting have become men of business and in some cases employers of labour . . .' It was a far cry from Webber, on the run from York Gaol, and Wilson, drilling in 1848 to these old buffers, placed in a humble station in the pantheon of Self-Help.[92]

---

91. Edward Owen Greening (1836–1923), who became a wire-cutter at the age of thirteen, was a key figure in the Co-operative movement for all of his adult life and had a particular interest in agricultural co-operatives. 1868 results: Stansfeld (L), 5,278; Akroyd (L), 5,141; Greening, 2,802.

92. *Halifax Courier*, 11 July 1885; Wilson, 'Struggles of an Old Chartist', in Vincent, *Testaments*, pp. 241–2; A. Taylor, 'Commemoration, Memorialisation and Political Memory in Post-Chartist Radicalism: The 1885 Halifax Chartist Reunion', in Ashton, Fyson and Roberts, *The Chartist Legacy*, pp. 255–85.

III

THE LEADERS OF THE PEOPLE

Invited, in the last year of her life, to choose her five favourite Chartists to appear on greetings cards, Dorothy Thompson made a selection that would not have surprised anyone who had ever discussed the Chartists with her: Feargus O'Connor; Bronterre O'Brien; Ernest Jones; John Frost; William Cuffay. The Irish-born leaders, the stalwarts of the West Riding, the insurrectionists and the women were the Chartists that Thompson most admired. Her empathy did not run so deep for the likes of William Lovett, Arthur O'Neill and Thomas Cooper, all of whom called themselves Chartists but did not support the leadership of O'Connor.

At the time that Thompson began thinking and writing about Chartism, O'Connor was seen as the chief villain of the movement. O'Connor had, in the words of Mark Hovell, 'debased the currency of Lovett, O'Brien and Benbow', and, in Neil Stewart's, 'led the movement to its doom'.[1] Thompson was unconvinced by this analysis,

---

1.   M. Hovell, *The Chartist Movement* (London, 1966 edn.), p. 195; N. Stewart, *The Fight for the Charter* (London, 1937). William Benbow played a significant part, as an editor and pamphleteer, in London radicalism in the 1830s.

finding it impossible to accept that a man with such
charisma, energy and resilience, a man who inspired so
much loyalty, could possibly be portrayed in such a
condemnatory way. The first piece in this section, originally published in 1952, suggested another way of looking
at O'Connor. While Thompson would later have refuted
her own suggestion that other Chartist leaders had a clearer
strategic view – and here she presumably meant O'Brien –
this short and overlooked essay was the first step on a
revisionist path that would lead to O'Connor's rehabilita-
tion, in a PhD thesis (and subsequently a book) by her
student James Epstein and then in her own monograph on
Chartism.

Four other leaders of the people are considered in this
section. The case is made for seeing John Fielden, the
factory owner who championed factory reform and who
addressed the great Chartist meetings in the north in 1838–
39, as a major figure. Though Thompson had once held the
view that Ernest Jones was 'a spellbinder' – and criticized
A. R. Schoyen for underestimating him in his biography of
Julian Harney – her admiration had contracted somewhat
over the years: although she recognized in Jones a tendency
to invention and duplicity, she still argued that his devotion
to the radical cause and the devotion of working people to
him overrode all of this. Harney is a rare example of a
Chartist who received his historical due early on; in the
piece in this section, Thompson welcomes Schoyen's
pioneering biography and also offers some interesting
observations about Harney's journalism. Finally, there is a
review of a biography of the middle-class reformer Joseph
Sturge who, in 1842, tried to forge a cross-class alliance by
seeking to persuade the Chartists to drop their Charter. It
could be argued that the book under review provided a
more useful discussion of this side of the radical movement
than Thompson acknowledged.

'THE MOST WELL-LOVED MAN': FEARGUS O'CONNOR

'The Lion of Freedom is come from his den / We'll rally around him again and again' – so sang the Chartists when, in their tens of thousands, they gathered to welcome Feargus O'Connor after his release from prison in 1841.[1] And when, six years later, he was elected a Member of Parliament for Nottingham, it must have seemed to the wealthy classes of England as though something far more dangerous than a roaring lion had been loosed in Westminster. For O'Connor, Chartist and repealer, was the most well-loved man in English public life during the forties of the nineteenth century.

For the Chartists, the 'unshorn chins and fustian jackets' of the northern manufacturing districts, O'Connor was the acknowledged leader of the movement. Abler men amongst the leadership there certainly were and men with a clearer sense of direction in which a working-class movement should go, but none of them had the appeal which O'Connor had nor his ability to win the confidence and support of the great crowds who made up the Chartist meetings in their heyday. Over six feet tall – he was almost the tallest man in

---

1. This piece was originally published in the *Irish Democrat*, September 1952.

the House of Commons – and with a voice which could easily carry at open-air meetings of tens of thousands, with a handsome appearance, a quick wit and a rich vein of scurrility when it came to abusing his opponents, O'Connor possessed all the qualities of the first-rate popular orator. He could stand up, moreover, to more than verbal opposition. Thomas Cooper describes an election meeting at which the opposition attacked in force. O'Connor disappeared for a time beneath a crowd of Tory toughs only to reappear after a short time, hitting out strongly, with a circle of them laid out all around him.[2] Such feats soon became well known throughout the factory districts, and he won a respect and affection accorded to few others in the whole of the century.

O'Connor was inspired in his Chartism by a hatred of the factory system. 'I have seen so much', he wrote, 'of the purse-proud Liberal masters, so much of the suffering of their slaves, both old and young, that I would cheerfully venture my life tomorrow to put an end to the damnable system, a system which, if not stopped, will snap every tie by which society should be bound.' The solution he held to lie in the People's Charter, which would give the vote under reasonably democratic conditions to every man in the kingdom, combined with a scheme of spade-tilled smallholdings, which would provide an alternative means of livelihood for the factory workers and so enable them to bargain for their labour power. 'I contend', he said, 'that no country can be considered prosperous or her people independent wherein the system of proprietorship of small farms and universal suffrage do not form the base of her social and political movement.'

O'Connor's first motion on being elected a Chartist MP was one for the repeal of the Act of Union between Great Britain and Ireland. He was a thoroughgoing repealer and

2. T. Cooper, *Life* (London, 1971 edn.), pp. 157–8; J. Epstein, 'Some Organisational and Cultural Aspects of the Chartist Movement in Nottingham', in Epstein and D. Thompson, *The Chartist Experience*, pp. 241–2.

had begun his political career before the Chartist movement existed as an Irish MP after the passing of the Catholic
emancipation. O'Connor's funeral in 1855 was the last of
the great gatherings of the Chartists. Although the movement was in decline, between fifty and sixty thousand
people met to pay their last tribute to the Irishman who had
led the English working class in the world's first political
labour movement.[3]

3. Pickering, *Feargus O'Connor*, p. 154.

10

'A RADICAL UNTIL THE END OF HIS DAYS': GEORGE JULIAN HARNEY

A.R. SCHOYEN, *THE CHARTIST CHALLENGE: A PORTRAIT OF GEORGE JULIAN HARNEY* (1958)
THE RED REPUBLICAN, REPRINT (1967)

A. R. Schoyen's book must in many ways be considered to be the first important work on Chartism.[1] In spite of its title, it is written as a straight biography of George Julian Harney, with very little moralizing and with its central figure placed firmly in his own intellectual and social context. Harney is a particularly good figure to take as central to the study of Chartism. For five years (1845–50) he was editor of the *Northern Star*. He was one of the few leading figures who entered the movement in its earliest days – coming in straight from an active part in the dramatic and principled fight against the stamp duties on newspapers which is one of the highlights of nineteenth-century radical action – and remained active throughout the years of its mass influence. He lived to a very great age, remaining a radical until the end of his days, and his biographer is spared the tedious task of chronicling any of the obscure byways, from phrenology to Unitarianism, into which so

---

1. This essay is made up of two pieces which appeared in the *New Reasoner* (Spring 1959), 138–41, and the *Bulletin of the Society for the Study of Labour History* 15 (1967), 28–33. Both pieces have been shortened.

many erstwhile Chartists penetrated after the end of the movement. What is more, although Harney had his share of policy disagreements with other leaders, he was a man without the great personal vanity which made O'Connor, O'Brien and others indulge in such bitter recrimination. W. E. Adams, the editor of the *Newcastle Weekly Chronicle*, who had grown up in the movement and had known most of its leaders, considered that 'no man had left behind so fair a record as George Julian Harney'.[2]

The correspondence of Marx and Engels during the active period of Chartism has been drawn upon by Schoyen quite extensively. However, the sharp, almost contemptuous tone of some of their references to Harney should probably not be taken too seriously. Their comments on Ernest Jones and other figures are also so sharp as to be almost bitter at times, but men like Harney and Jones were personal friends, and it must be remembered that the letters were written usually in great political excitement and were, in any case, exchanged in privacy between two very close friends. Certainly, in spite of the waspish tone of some of their references to Harney, he continued to admire them both and to maintain a friendly correspondence with them. In 1885 he was still writing to Engels, who contributed a pathetic picture of the old Chartist in a letter to Paul Lafarge:

> I had a letter last week from old Harney; he sailed the 12th October, much too late for his condition of body, and, of course, arrived rheumatic and gouty all over . . . Poor fellow – when the Chartist movement broke down he found himself adrift . . . He went to Boston, only to find there, in an exaggerated form and ruling supreme, those very things and qualities which he hated most in England. And now when a real movement begins on both sides of the Atlantic

---

2.   W. E. Adams, *Memoirs of a Social Atom* (London, 1903), p. 218. Adams (1832–1906) was active in late Chartism in Cheltenham, and, from 1864 until 1900, edited the *Newcastle Weekly Chronicle*. See O. R. Ashton, *W. E. Adams: Chartist, Radical and Journalist* (Whitley Bay, 1991).

amongst the English-speaking nations, he is too old, too decrepit, too much an outsider and too patriotic to follow it. All he has learnt in America is British chauvinism.

Harney was, above all, a journalist. His following in the movement was amongst the thoughtful, younger members – men like Thomas Frost and W. E. Adams, young printers, aspiring journalists themselves, who saw in his republicanism, internationalism and iconoclastically rational approach to all institutions something which went beyond the bread-and-butter Chartism of some of the older leaders.[3] For several months in 1850 Harney edited the *Red Republican*. It was a curious production. Harney was undoubtedly at his best when working on a publication that was not inhibited by newspaper taxes from printing and commenting on current news. Under his editorship the *Star* was one of the great newspapers of the nineteenth century, but his personally-produced journals, from the *London Democrat* (1839) to the *Northern Tribune* (1854–55) never approached the level achieved in the sort of publication produced by O'Brien or even by Jones.

Harney published his side of the various quarrels surrounding his break with O'Connor in the *Red Republican*. The story of this break has been that Harney worked on the *Star* until his differences with O'Connor became so great, particularly in relation to the paper's treatment of foreign affairs, that he was forced to resign. In fact it appears rather more likely that Harney decided to break away from the *Star* because of its declining circulation and the dramatic decline in the standing of O'Connor himself. It had always been possible for an editorial team representing a variety of views to work together on the *Star*, and there is no doubt that being its editor gave Harney an important position in the movement. In 1850 the position of editor of a paper

---

3. Thomas Frost (1821–1908), a Croydon Chartist who was present at the Kennington Common demonstration of April 1848, was employed as a correspondent for many provincial newspapers. His reminiscences (1880 and 1886) are of real interest.

with only a fraction of its former circulation was no longer one which appeared to carry prestige and influence, and Harney decided to try and gain a following, particularly amongst the foreign refugees and the Chartists with an international outlook, by publishing a journal which was mainly concerned with European affairs.

The *Red Republican* was one of a proliferation of small, personal, unstamped journals which appeared in the years after 1848. In a way they represent an unscrambling of the coalition that had been Chartism, and in them can be found some of the best Chartist writing on non-immediate questions – O'Brien on the 'Rise and Fall of Human Slavery' and W. J. Vernon on prison discipline in *Reynolds's Political Instructor*, Jones's prison poems in his *Notes to the People*, O'Connor's incomplete autobiography in the *National Instructor*, W. J. Linton on republicanism in the *English Republic*, G. J. Holyoake on secularism in the *Reasoner*, and many others.[4] The *Red Republican* contains Harney on European revolutions, and contributions from some of the émigré leaders, including Ledru-Rollin and Louis Blanc. But Harney's internationalism is of a curious quality. It contains more of the romantic search for heroes than a sense of sympathy with the working people of other countries. It is easy to understand the frustration of Marx and Engels, who nicknamed him 'Citizen Hip Hip Hurrah', perhaps after reading one of his poems with the chorus:

> Then sing brothers sing,
> Let the loud chorus ring,
> All men are brethren! Hip! Hip! Hurrah!

---

4. W. J. Vernon offered his services as a mesmerist in London before taking up the Chartist cause in 1848: see A. Winter, *Mesmerized: Powers of Mind in Victorian Britain* (Cambridge, 1999), pp. 125–7, 138–9, 156–8; W. J. Linton, an engraver backed by funds from the wealthy Newcastle radical Joseph Cowen, operated a printing press in the Lake District and published the *English Republic* (1851–55) and the *Northern Tribune* (1854); G. J. Holyoake absorbed the *Northern Tribune* into his secularist journal, the *Reasoner* (1846–61); he subsequently wrote for Cowen's hugely successful *Newcastle Daily Chronicle*, amongst other newspapers.

An internationalist who never learned a foreign language, who opposed Home Rule for Ireland, and who complained that the plunder from the Indian Empire was not fairly divided amongst the population of Britain, Harney, divorced from the *Star* and with little effective contact with a movement in a country, appears at his least impressive. It is not as a theoretician, or even primarily as a writer of good journalism, that Harney's importance lies, but as the editor of the *Star* and as one of the organizers and speakers of the movement when it was at its height.

11

'THE BEST-REMEMBERED CHARTIST': ERNEST JONES

MILES TAYLOR, *ERNEST JONES, CHARTISM AND THE ROMANCE OF POLITICS 1819–69* (OXFORD, 2003)

Chartism was a movement whose members, supporters, and most of its leaders, were working men. A few were shopkeepers, innkeepers or marginal members of lesser professions.[1] Such people rarely leave family archives, and so almost all that we know about them comes from the press, prison records or published reminiscences. An exception to this is Ernest Jones, who left behind many personal papers including a diary, a large number of letters and copious notes of his financial affairs and of his work as an editor, speaker and later a barrister on the Northern Circuit. It is therefore surprising that Miles Taylor's is the first full-length biography of Jones – the more so since he is the best-remembered of the Chartist leaders, among the pioneers of the modern Labour movement and a friend of both Marx and Engels.

The legend that has survived Jones after his early death in 1869 was of a poet who, as a young man, had cast aside comfort and wealth to take part in the movement of the working people. He had been arrested in the year of revolutions, 1848, and had served two years in prison, where he

---

1. This review was originally published in the *Times Higher Education Supplement*, 5 December 2003.

had been refused paper and books and had written inspiring poems in his own blood. On his release in 1850 he had fought desperately to keep the ailing Chartist movement alive, and had finally made his peace with radical Liberalism. He died on the eve of his election to the House of Commons. At least this was the story passed on by such early twentieth-century socialists as Ben Turner and Charles Glyde, and by G. D. H Cole in his *Chartist Portraits*. The biographical introduction to a selection of Jones's writing edited by John Saville in 1952 did not significantly alter the legend.[2]

A closer examination of the material, however, shows that the Jones legend was largely his own invention. He did come from a minor gentry family, but not one from which he had serious hopes of inheriting wealth. His desire for a career as a man of letters was not matched by his ability as an editor or as a writer of verse or prose. He came into the Chartist movement with some romantic enthusiasm at a time when it was already in decline or spreading into more limited movements such as trade unionism or co-operation. His story is not one of great radical political success, but of an unsuccessful search for a career in politics and letters. As such, it is of great interest to anyone wanting to understand some of the realities of life in the mid-Victorian period.

Taylor has written an immensely readable account, putting straight the record about some of Jones's romantic claims without debunking or ridiculing the man himself. Jones did put in years of work for radical causes and earned the loyalty and respect of many Chartists. If he also quarrelled with many of his colleagues and was always unreliable in matters of money, he did not become rich at the movement's expense. A few of his verses were remembered and sold as street ballads. His Gothic prose fiction is best forgotten. Taylor does not add much to our knowledge of Chartism and its leaders; but this story of the efforts, ambitions and family life of an unsuccessful seeker after a literary career helps to fill out our knowledge of the age.

---

2. B. Turner, *Yorkshire Factory Times*, 23 January 1919; C. Glyde, *Bradford Socialist Vanguard*, February 1919; Saville, *Ernest Jones*.

12

'TWO OF THE MOST INFLUENTIAL OF RADICAL VOICES': JOHN FIELDEN AND JOSEPH STURGE

STEWART ANGUS WEAVER, *JOHN FIELDEN AND THE POLITICS OF POPULAR RADICALISM 1832–1847* (OXFORD, 1987)

ALEX TYRELL, *JOSEPH STURGE AND THE MORAL RADICAL PARTY IN EARLY VICTORIAN BRITAIN* (1987)

The years between the end of the French wars and the middle of the nineteenth century were a time when, as George Eliot recalled , 'faith in the efficacy of political change was at fever-heat in ardent reformers'.[1] It is surprising that two of the most influential of the radical voices to be heard in those years have had to wait for so long for scholarly biographies. John Fielden (1784–1849), senior partner and chief administrator in the world's largest cotton firm, was one of the originators of the Chartist movement and a lifelong campaigner for legal measures to protect the hours, conditions and rewards of workers in industry.[2] Joseph Sturge (1793–1859) was a wealthy

---

1. G. Eliot, *Felix Holt, the Radical* (London, 1866), p. 162. This essay was published in the *Times Literary Supplement*, 11 December 1987. This version omits most of the introductory paragraph and slightly reduces the penultimate paragraph.

2. Fielden Brothers came into being in 1803 when Joshua Fielden (1748–1811) of Todmorden retired from running his spinning mills; though the third son, John Fielden had worked closely with his father, both in the mills and on business trips, and oversaw the considerable expansion of the business.

Quaker and corn dealer, a leading publicist of the anti-slavery movement, a pacifist and temperance advocate and at times a campaigner for adult male suffrage.[3] Fielden has been the subject of work by local historians in his native Todmorden, Sturge has been celebrated in two hagiographies and both were included in G. D. H. Cole's *Chartist Portraits*.[4] The two volumes under review, however, represent the first full-length modern studies.

Weaver deals primarily with Fielden the politician. By limiting his scope in this way, he is able to produce in a restricted space a detailed account of one of the most misunderstood figures in radical politics. *John Fielden and the Politics of Popular Radicalism 1832–1847* is a model of its kind, compulsively readable, thoroughly documented, with footnotes where they should be, at the foot of the page. Fielden emerges as a character of considerable stature and strong principles. A rich – at times extremely rich – man, he spent his time, energy and a considerable part of his fortune attempting, through parliamentary means, to have controls placed on the industrial system of which he was a leading representative. In an age in which radicals held that political power was the key to social improvement, he believed that legal intervention could ensure that industrialization would benefit the entire community.

A free-trader in most economic matters, he did not extend these principles to the labour market or to human relations in general. His proposals for trade boards and a minimum wage for handloom weavers, like his opposition to the 1834 Poor Law Amendment Act and its implementation, or his agitation for a ten-hour working day for factories, were based on his knowledge of industry and the industrial communities and were opposed to the dogmas of academic political economy. In Parliament he differed from

---

3.   Sturge's money came from a hugely successful grain-importing business which, after 1831, was run by his brother Charles whilst he concentrated on his philanthropic and political activities.

4.   H. Richard, *Memoirs of Joseph Sturge* (London, 1864); J. Hobhouse, *Joseph Sturge* (London, 1919); J. Holden, *A Short History of Todmorden* (Manchester, 1912).

nearly all his fellow radicals in his consistent refusal to be drawn into siding with either of the two political parties.[5]

A supporter of radical causes up to and during the early years of the Chartist movement, he withdrew somewhat after the events of 1839–40, though never disavowing Chartism. He remained on friendly terms with O'Connor and other leading Chartists and was always ready to defend those who were arrested and to present petitions to the House of Commons. He introduced a motion for repeal of the Act of Union with Ireland early in his parliamentary career and consistently opposed every coercion bill.

Even more than Thomas Slingsby Duncombe and Thomas Wakley, two other Chartist MPs, Fielden spoke consciously for extra-parliamentary radicalism and for the interests of labour as he saw them. What is more, in his active opposition to the implementation of the New Poor Law in his own part of Lancashire, he employed and advocated tactics of mass demonstration and the withdrawal of labour which were those of the most militant Chartists. Weaver offers a perceptive and convincing examination of the tactics and rhetoric of the popular radicalism of these years that could hardly be bettered, and in so doing places John Fielden where he belongs, among its major figures.

Alex Tyrrell's *Joseph Sturge and the Moral Radical Party in Early Victorian Britain* suffers to some extent by comparison. The book is cut up into very short chapters and is remorselessly confined to the viewpoint of its subject. Tyrrell seems on too many occasions to accept his subject's moralism at face value. The picture of the Anti-Corn Law Leaguers reduced to inarticulacy by tears when describing working-class living conditions is singularly unconvincing, given their attitudes in other circumstances. As Weaver shows, the lachrymose John Bright was one of the chief

---

5. Fielden was elected, with William Cobbett, as one of the two MPs for Oldham in 1832. He steered through the 1847 Factory Act, of which Stewart A. Weaver, in the *Oxford Dictionary of National Biography* (London, 2004), observed, 'More than the great moment of Fielden's life, it was the turning point of an age, the first significant admission of governmental responsibility for the welfare of the working poor.'

exponents of the legal limitation of child labour in factories. Sturge was a more consistent and attractive figure than
Bright, but he still emerges from this study as self-
righteous. Like Fielden, he was extremely rich – 'Have you
a California of your own?' Cobden once asked him, perhaps
with a touch of envy – but we are given little information
about his political use of funds. No mention is made, for
example, of his use of money to establish alternative groups
to mainstream Chartists in Birmingham, although 'Sturge
milk' – to use one Chartist's phrase – undoubtedly tempted
more than one hard-up activist into the Sturge camp.

Although he stood for Parliament on several occasions,
Sturge never became an MP. He tended to look higher for
possibilities of political influence, to approach members of
the government directly and even, on occasion, heads of
state, including the Tsar.[6] In his last decade, in the jingoistic
years surrounding the Crimean War, much of his influence
was exercised on behalf of the Peace Society. He laid out a
great deal of money and effort in helping to found and
support a daily newspaper, the *Morning Star*, to carry the
message of Christian pacifism. It would be interesting to
have a fuller account of these years. Alex Tyrrell might have
been better advised to expand some sections of his work,
rather than attempt the impossible task of covering all the
many interests and activities of his subject in a short book.[7]

---

6. Sturge stood for election in Nottingham in 1842, Birmingham in
1847 and Leeds in 1847, being defeated on each occasion. His meeting with
the Tsar took place in January 1854 as part of a delegation sent to Russia
by the Society of Friends.

7. Also see reviews by T. R. Tholfsen, *Albion* 20:1 (1988); G. Finlayson,
Victorian Studies 31:4 (1988); R. Sykes, *Bulletin of the Society for the
Study of Labour* History, 53:3 (1988).

IV

REPERCUSSIONS

This section begins with the final essay Dorothy Thompson wrote – her thoughts on that great year of upheaval, 1848. The essay is a largely unrevised paper presented at a conference on radicalism and nationalism across Britain and Ireland in the half-century following the 1798 United Irish rebellion, held at the University of Aberdeen in July 1999. It is a somewhat unpolished piece and can perhaps be seen as Thompson 'talking to herself, thinking aloud and clarifying her own, sometimes revised (now ex-Marxist) views on a subject she had been thinking about for many years'.[1] Nonetheless it does reaffirm her important argument that, if Chartism ever represented an insurrectionary threat, it was in 1839–40, and also explains why it was that the Chartists and the Irish leaders were unable to make common cause in 1848. Thompson was most likely drawn to the theme by the publication of a monograph by John Saville.

As with Thompson's own book-length discussion of Chartism, *1848: The British State and the Chartist Movement* (1987) was the culmination of a lifetime of research, thinking and rethinking. Saville had been

---

1. R. Fyson to S. Roberts, 20 November 2012.

interested in countering the entrenched view that Chartism fizzled out ingloriously on the famous 10 April and in examining how the authorities dealt with the very real threat of an organized and national campaign to enfranchise working men since he first began writing. When it finally appeared, Saville's long-gestated book extended the discussion to Ireland and responded emphatically to the assertion of Stedman Jones that the state was proving itself responsive to the interests of working people. For these reasons, he might have expected a supportive review from his long-standing scholarly (and political) ally, Thompson. In a long and closely-argued review, however, Thompson took issue with Saville's argument. Having suggested that Saville's research on Irish sources was too narrow – he had apparently not examined journals such as the *Nation* and the *United Irishman* – Thompson argued that he was incorrect to suggest that events in France, Ireland and Britain were in phase. On Irish politics, on which she had thought deeply, and in her observation that Saville had little to say about what happened – or in fact didn't happen – outside London, Thompson's criticisms were surely legitimate. Taking stock of Saville's book a quarter of a century after its publication, Malcolm Chase rallied to its defence. He accepted Saville's contention that there was an intersection between events in France, Ireland and Britain and found himself – more than once – using the term 'powerful' in evaluating the book.[2] Whilst Thompson had provided the most penetrating and passionately-engaged review of Saville's book, she had perhaps not given enough credit to the real depth of his research in the papers of the ruling elite, or to his attempts to respond comprehensively to Stedman Jones's arguments or to break new ground in exploring the Irish dimension. Buttressed by formidable footnotes, *1848* is, indisputably, a notable contribution to the historiography of Chartism.[3]

---

2. Chase, 'The Chartist Movement and 1848', in Howell, Kirby and Morgan, *John Saville*, pp. 155–74.

3. See G. A. Williams, *Guardian*, 25 September 1987.

This section concludes with Thompson's reviews of two books which were published in the 1990s on what happened to the radical agenda after 1848. She welcomed Margot Finn's reassertion of the importance of class in *After Chartism: Class and Nation in English Radical Politics, 1848–1874* (1993), and indeed her chapter discussing the genealogy of English radicalism received the very rare Thompsonian accolade of 'brilliant'. Meanwhile, Thompson's detection that Miles Taylor's *The Decline of British Radicalism 1847–1860* (1995) was 'topped up . . . by the incorporating of the insights of the "linguistic turn"' was certain to guarantee it the most testing of interrogations.

13

THE CHARTISTS IN 1848

This essay takes as its standpoint 1848 – a year that left a number of important markers in European history.[1] Later in the century it came to be known as 'the year of revolutions', and there were indeed risings in many parts of the Continent. It was also the year of the publication of the *Communist Manifesto* which, for good or ill, began an era in which revolutionary politics acquired a new significance. It proved to be almost midway between the two revolutions of 1789 and 1917, which shaped modern European history. It is not surprising therefore that 1848 is recalled as a year of important events and important decisions. In looking at what happened in England in that year of revolutions, I want to consider some of the various views of contemporaries and of historians; and to reflect on some of the interpretations and re-interpretations of British popular politics in that year and in the century as a whole.

To begin with, then, what did happen? The various movements which had emerged in Europe since the defeat

---

1. This essay was first published in T. Brotherstone, A. Clark and K. Whelan, eds, *These Fissured Isles: Ireland, Scotland and British History, 1798–1848* (Edinburgh, 2005), pp. 165–77. Inaccuracies in quotations have been corrected, and the text has been slightly shortened.

of Napoleon in 1815 had begun to follow a definite pattern. The Napoleonic Wars had increased the strength of nationalism in most parts of the Continent, and with that came the demand for discrete nation states based on ethnic divisions. The nations that were emerging sought to throw off the rule of the old imperial powers and also in many cases to modernize their forms of government. Republics and constitutionally limited monarchies were in favour – in many cases partly modelled on the British constitution. The Romantic movement in the arts was often allied with the new nationalist and republican sentiments, although, of course, there was also a strongly traditionalist element in much of its discourse.

In England the years since the end of the wars had seen the emergence of political reform as a driving force in popular politics. By the beginning of the 1830s major successes had been achieved by the new extra-parliamentary reform movements. First, there was the abolition in 1828 of the Tests and Corporation Acts; then the achievement in 1829 of Catholic emancipation; and, above all, in 1832 the passing of the Reform Act, by which holders of forms of property other than land were admitted to the franchise. All these important constitutional acts had been achieved by a combination of parliamentary compromise enforced by extra-parliamentary action. A House of Commons, from which Catholics were totally excluded, had passed Catholic emancipation; a House of Commons filled with the nominees of landed proprietors had passed the bill that enfranchised other forms of property. As the Duke of Wellington put it, the revolution had begun and the government of the country had been taken out of the hands of landed gentlemen and members of the Church of England and handed over to 'the shopkeepers . . . many them being Socinians, others atheists'.[2] The 1832 Act established a franchise based more exclusively on clearly defined property ownership than any before it. It is true that even

---

2. Quoted in R. B. McDowell, *British Conservatism 1832–1914* (London, 1959), p. 18.

propertied women did not get the franchise, the age for
voting was twenty-one and the registration for the franchise demanded a settled period of residence; but,
nevertheless, this was the widest franchise in Europe and
the elected parliament had fewer constraints on its actions
than almost any other. Britain was on the road to becoming
a bourgeois democracy.

I have rehearsed this well-known background to enable
me to make comparisons between the revolutionary drives
in continental Europe and those – if there were any – in
Britain. The use of the term 'Britain' is of course deliberate,
because, although there were legal and political differences
between the systems in England, Scotland and Wales, these
were not much in evidence in these years. Ireland, however,
was another matter, to which I return below.

I.

The reform movement in Britain in 1848 was Chartism.
The original People's Charter was a proposal for a bill to be
introduced in Parliament based on the famous 'Six Points'.
This programme was not new. It had been formulated
during the eighteenth century and most of it had been put
forward during the agitation for the Reform Act of 1832.
The form of petition to Parliament was also traditional:
non-electors as well as electors had the right to do this, and
many thousands of petitions had been presented over the
years. The Chartist petition, however, was new in that it
was national: it took the same form in all parts of the country. It was also to be backed by simultaneous meetings of
support throughout the country and by a National
Convention – or anti-parliament – to supervise its organization, collection and presentation. The National Petition
of 1839 was a detailed proposal for a bill to reform the
voting and electoral system, even giving details of the sort
of ballot box to be used. The National Petition of 1842
added repeal of the New Poor Law and of the Act of Union,
and was presented in a year of strikes and lockouts – of

industrial as well as political action throughout the manufacturing districts.

By 1848, then, we can see an organized campaign for
change which had no parallel in the rest of Europe, with the
possible exception of France, where there was an urban
artisan movement – particularly in Paris – with some of the
characteristics of Chartism.[3] In Britain, moreover, the
issues were expressed in political terms. These were years,
as George Eliot wrote, looking back from the 1860s, 'when
faith in the efficacy of political change was at fever-heat in
ardent reformers'.[4] Those who took part in the widespread popular movement undoubtedly had grievances that
could better be described as 'social' rather than 'political'.
They included low and declining wages; the break-up of the
family caused by the factory system and the provisions of
the New Poor Law; the advent of provincial police forces,
which interfered with popular recreations and political
activities; and many others common to most industrializing
countries. But in Britain the road to reform was seen to lie
through the enlargement of the political system to include
the working class, not the overthrow of the system as such.

It is at this point that we come to some of the problems
with the interpretation of the British experience and its
comparison with the rest of Europe. In most of Europe the
revolutions of 1848 were concerned with the end of *anciens
régimes*, and with the break-up of the old empires. The
British *ancien régime* had fallen without violence in 1832.
Insofar as the rights of the small nations against imperial
dominion were at issue in Britain, it was the Irish, and, at a
greater distance, the people of the Indian subcontinent who
were concerned: Britain itself was the ruling empire. In a
country such as Poland there was a widely-based nationalist stance which included Roman Catholics and
Polish-speakers of all classes. In England, where many of

---

3.   I. J. Prothero, *Radical Artisans in England and France, 1830–1870*
(Cambridge, 1998). Thompson found this book 'absorbing and
enlightening': see *Times Higher Education Supplement*, 17 April 1998, for
her review.
4.   Eliot, *Felix Holt*, chap. 26.

the nationalist movements had their émigré support groups, there were several Polish nationalist groups, only one of which liaised with the Chartists.[5] Most of the cross-class groups that included aristocratic and landowning nationalist groups had no time for the democratic politics of English workmen. To a degree this applied to most of the European nationalists in exile. The Chartists cheered for Kossuth, Mazzini and Garibaldi, and in many provincial and well as metropolitan centres supported refugees from Europe. In 1845 they founded the Fraternal Democrats, a London-based society in which refugees and artisan nationalists from all over Europe held discussions, had regular meetings and issued appeals to the democracy of Europe. The words 'foreign' and 'foreigner' were discouraged, if not forbidden, at their meetings. Nevertheless, most of the European nationalist movements were far less concerned with democracy than with nationhood. Ireland, in many ways, illustrates the question.

Ireland had been occupied by Britain for many centuries, but towards the end of the eighteenth century a degree of autonomy had begun to emerge. The Irish movement for independence had something in common with the American at this stage, in that the political leadership involved many figures from the families of plantation settlers – including many Protestants who were chafing at British rule. The 1798 rising included many Irishmen and women from both the Protestant and Catholic communities. Castlereagh described it as 'a Jacobinical conspiracy . . . pursuing its object chiefly with Popish instruments'.[6] It was defeated and put down with draconian ferocity by the British. Many 'United men' emigrated or were transported and became early members of the British, American and Australian democratic movements. Many Irishmen in Britain in 1848 were from United families, some even survivors of the '98

---

5.   This was the Democratic Committee for the Regeneration of Poland, launched in 1846 and effectively a subsidiary of the Fraternal Democrats: see A. R. Schoyen, pp. 139–40.
6.   Quoted in W. Hinde, *Castlereagh* (London, 1981), p. 64.

themselves. Feargus O'Connor was the nephew of one of the leaders of the rising, Arthur O'Connor, and the son of another United man, Roger. Feargus gave to the Chartist newspaper he established the name the *Northern Star*, which came from the United Irish paper of the 1790s.

The repeal of the Act of Union had been on the agenda of all working-class political reform movements in Britain since the end of the French wars. In fact it was one of the demands that distinguished these movements from reform movements among the middle and upper classes.

After the 1798 rising, outrageous bribery and some coercion bought out the Irish Parliament and the Act of Union was passed. From that point Ireland had been governed largely by coercion. In 1848 its relationship to Britain could be compared with the nationalities still under the rule of the Russian and Austro-Hungarian empires. The Chartists in fact often used the comparison. In 1848 Ernest Jones wrote of Ireland:

> Why weeps your sorrowing sister,
> Still bleeding, unredressed,
> 'Neath Russell, England's Nicholas,
> The Poland of the West?[7]

The British working people, then, felt themselves oppressed and exploited and looked to a solution of manhood suffrage, which would make Parliament responsive to their needs. For Ireland they also proposed manhood suffrage, but this was to be combined with national liberation, represented by the repeal of the Act of Union.

The Irish nationalist movement that had grown up in the years before 1848 was, however, very different in character from the United Irishmen. Its leader Daniel O'Connell had served as a volunteer against the rebels of 1798. He was not a republican, believing in the Crown as a 'golden bridge' between the two nations. He had been amongst the Catholic leaders who gave an effusive welcome to George IV on his

---

7. *Northern Star*, 18 March 1848.

visit to Ireland in 1823. And he gained enormous popularity by his skilful political tactics in 1829, when he earned
the sobriquet 'The Liberator' by successfully challenging
the Government and achieving Catholic emancipation.
O'Connell was probably the national leader who earned
the greatest following in Ireland during the nineteenth
century. He was one of the great orators of the century and
could attract huge crowds wherever he went. But he relied
for support and finance on the backing of the Catholic
Church; and the Church was ambivalent about separation
from Britain, much preferring the idea that Britain as a
whole might be regained for the true faith, an outcome that
too harsh a break might prejudice.

The Chartists in 1848, then, had two main agendas. One
was an anti-imperial agenda: at home, freedom for Ireland;
in Europe, support for nationalist struggle against the
Russian and Austro-Hungarian empires. Within Britain the
programme was for political reform, driven by those who
had been excluded from the franchise in 1832, that is, all
who lived in property worth less than £10 a year. The
Chartists described themselves as working-class – the rhetoric of class was widespread in Britain when Engels arrived
there in 1844 – and also used expressions like 'the productive classes' or 'the useful classes'. These latter terms were
sometimes held to include manufacturers of useful commod-
ities, but were generally used to mean those who worked
but were excluded from the franchise.

2.

An important argument is whether Chartism was in fact a
class movement. Some historians point to the use of constitutional rhetoric which they see as supporting a nationalistic
(or 'populist') rather than a class analysis. The Chartists
did indeed sometimes look back to a time when the constitution was 'pure' – referring to the Anglo Saxon *witenagemot*
where all adult men voted by raising their hands. The overturning of the pure English constitution by the invading

Normans, who went on to form an overbearing non-native aristocracy, had been part of the popular mythology of England for many years, as Christopher Hill demonstrated.[8] It was one of the many elements in the rhetoric of popular politics. There were other national myths: Boadicea defending the British against the Romans, King Alfred as the epitome of Englishness, for example. Samuel Kydd, a leading Chartist in 1848, in fact used the pseudonym 'Alfred' when he published his substantial history of the factory movement in 1857.[9] Britain was, moreover, a Protestant nation in which every household had access to the Bible, and biblical rhetoric was a powerful part of the language which unified a country which was still very regional and contained many different dialects. In 1839 Henry Vincent had been imprisoned for a speech in which the phrase 'To your tents, O Israel' was interpreted as incitement to rebellion. The Bible was used to test the literacy of people who were arrested and the Chartists often rejoiced in selecting favourite texts – 'ye rich men, weep and howl for your miseries that shall come on you' – as their test. Classical texts which had been encountered at grammar schools and Shakespeare were, as Henry Mayhew noted, very popular in the penny gaffs frequented by the London costermongers. They were often presented by barnstorming companies in inn yards. The Leicester Chartists indeed called themselves the 'Shakespearean Association'.[10] There was also a host of stories and ballads from chapbooks and broadsides, nursery rhymes and tales of witches, fairies and such – many of which survived only as very bowdlerized children's stories. All of these were part of a national store of images and languages which could override local dialect and gave the Chartists a national vocabulary among the common people. The fact that there was also a strong rhetoric of class is not a contradiction.

---

8. C. Hill, 'The Norman Yoke', in J. Saville, ed., *Democracy and the Labour Movement: Essays in Honour of Dona Torr* (London, 1954).
9. For Kydd see Roberts, *Radical Politicians and Poets*, pp. 107–27.
10. See Roberts, *The Chartist Prisoners*, pp. 72–80.

Many of the Chartist songs and poems were sung to traditional folk tunes or other popular melodies. Chartist hymns were written to accepted tunes and in hymn style:

> Rouse them from their silken slumbers,
> Trouble them amidst their pride;
> Swell your ranks, augment your numbers,
> Spread the Charter far and wide!
> Truth is with us:
> God Himself is on our side.[11]

The fact that at many points the movement used the language and the imagery of popular, literate culture reinforces the movement's class nature rather than undermining it. The 'language of class' was far broader than what used to be seen as politically correct within the terminology of 'scientific socialism'.

The disagreement between historians about Chartism in 1848 is illustrated by the work of Gareth Stedman Jones and John Saville. To simplify the argument, it is about whether Chartism in that year was the end of a long radical tradition going back into the eighteenth century, or the beginning of a class-based movement which was to lead to modern revolutionary labour politics. In other words, was 1848 in Britain in effect a failed revolution or was it the artificially revived end of an old political tradition? The Chartist revival in the winter of 1847–8 was undoubtedly widespread and on a considerable scale. The organization had remained in existence after the trials of O'Connor and others in 1843, but activity had been low-key. Stedman Jones suggests that a Tory regime under Peel liberalized aspects of state policy, particularly in matters of taxation, and thereby relieved the fears of exploitation and authoritarian control among the population. Saville, on the other hand, proposes that, far from liberalizing the state, the Tories set up an efficient system of policing and used new developments in

---

11. Cooper, *Life*, p. 167.

communications such as railways and telegraphs to maintain increased vigilance and control.

My own view differs from both Stedman Jones's and Saville's. The high point of Chartism, in my view, came in the years 1838–40. The government after January 1840 did not enforce draconian punishment. A number of points exemplify this. That month the death sentences on the leaders of the Newport Rising were commuted. The provisions of the New Poor Law were not implemented in their totality: outdoor relief in fact continued in the manufacturing districts. The 1839 Rural Police Act was enforced only in a very cautious and local way. The edge was thus taken off the defensive side of the movement. This led many to turn to other forms of defence, starting emigration societies, building new trade unions and experimenting with co-operative production and trading societies. This kind of local non-political work was, in most cases, begun and carried on by Chartists and did not imply the rejection of the political route – indeed many of those involved were to re-emerge in the campaign for the 1867 Reform Act. It did, however, lower the priority of political change; and, of course, these working-class institutions came to represent something of a vested interest when violent or all-out action might be called for. The repeal of the Corn Laws in 1846 and the passing of the 1847 Factory Act may have seemed also to have been concessions to extra-parliamentary pressure, and achieved without the suffrage.

Ireland, however, saw no concessions or liberalization. From 1845 the grievances of colonial oppression were reinforced by the agony of famine. The nationalist movement had been slow to attack the Whigs with whom O'Connell formed an alliance in 1835. With the return of the Tories in 1841, however, O'Connell founded the Loyal National Repeal Association (LNRA), the first item of whose membership requirement was an oath of loyalty to the Queen. He refused to have anything to do with the Irish Universal Suffrage Association (IUSA) – the Irish Chartists – and forbade joint membership. There were, therefore, by the mid-1840s two movements advocating repeal of the

Union: O'Connell's massive LNRA, funded with the co-operation of the Catholic Church; and the IUSA, with small groups in artisan centres including Dublin, working in co-operation with the British Chartists. Ireland, as I have suggested, was in many ways like the countries of continental Europe, which were to see revolutions in France and Germany. The differences included the famine experience and the enforced rejection of the artisan radicals who formed an important part of the movements in France and Germany.[12]

In England itself the argument that 1848 was a revolutionary year rests not so much on empirical evidence as on Marxist teleology. Given that bourgeois freedom had largely been attained, the next stage, the argument went, had to be proletarian revolution. From his correspondence with Harney, it seems that Engels in 1846 expected a working-class revolution in Britain, the Charter before the end of the decade and the abolition of private property by the end of the century. Harney had his doubts.[13]

Does a class analysis of Chartism require the acceptance of this teleological Marxism? If it does, the big problems of Chartism include the question of why there was not a revolution in Britain in 1848 and of what happened to the undoubtedly high level of class consciousness that existed during the decade from 1838 to 1848. The latter question has often been explained by a theoretical construct known as the 'aristocracy of labour'. This is the idea that the natural leaders of the working class – the skilled workmen – were 'bought off' by the spoils of imperialism and the exploitation of subject nations; and that they thereby became comfortable with capitalism and neglected their less fortunate brothers among the unskilled. The British skilled workers, unlike their continental brethren, did not adopt a Marxist analysis of the route to social improvement and

---

12. See D. Thompson, 'Ireland and the Irish in English Radicalism before 1850', in Epstein and Thompson, *The Chartist Experience*, pp. 120–51.

13. F. G. Black and R. M. Black, eds, *The Harney Papers* (Assen, 1969), pp. 239–40.

instead adopted reformist policies or accommodation with capitalism. By this analysis the offer of palliatives by government, employers and the state deflected the raw class conflict that existed at the heart of the system and so prevented the revolution and its projected outcome of a better society.

Stedman Jones sought to attack the 'aristocracy of labour' theory. If, as he suggests, the motives behind Chartism were entirely political, then the liberalization of the British state and the lifting of some of the burden of taxation meant that politics ceased to be important and the political movement died away. But Saville's contradictory claim has some justice. The state, he insists, far from being liberalized, became much tougher in its treatment of dissidence. It faced the Chartists with strong policing and the threat of the military, and this led to the collapse of the movement's leadership. Had their leaders given the signal for insurrection, this argument suggests, the Chartists and the Irish would have risen and overthrown the capitalist state.

When this argument is baldly set out in this way, it answers itself. In Ireland, the effects of the famine and the hostility to class-based analysis among the nationalist leaders made meaningful co-operation with the Chartists out of the question. When, in 1847, the Young Ireland group split with O'Connell on the question of the use of arms to achieve Ireland's liberation from Britain, they did not move towards an alliance with the Chartists until it was too late. Their call for a rising in Ireland produced a turnout of between two and three hundred, followed by the transportation of their leaders. Even though the revolution in France in February 1848 had given them some encouragement, as it had to the Chartists, the artisans of Paris were not seen by them as natural allies. John Mitchel wrote in his *Jail Journal* in late 1848: 'In June . . . the "Red Republicans" and Communists attempted another Paris revolution, which, if successful, would have been a horrible affair . . . but they were swept from the streets by grape and canister – the only way of dealing with such unhappy creatures.'[14]

---

14.   J. Mitchel, *Jail Journal, 1876* (Glasgow, 1876), p. 86.

3.

To the Irish nationalists, then, the revolution in France was encouraging only as an attack on authority. They had sympathy neither with its democrats nor its anti-clerical elements. For the Chartists, however, it was a tremendous invigoration of their third campaign for the Charter that had, by February, been going on for several months. Throughout the country working people welcomed the revolution. Resolutions were passed and addresses sent to the French people. In Yorkshire thousands attended an open-air camp meeting and greeted the revolution with a Chartist hymn:

> Britannia's sons, though slaves ye be,
> God your Creator made you free;
> He, life and thought and being gave,
> But never, never, made a slave!
> . . .
> All men are equal in His sight,
> The bond, the free, the black, the white;
> He made them all, them freedom gave,
> *He* made the man – *Man made the slave!*[15]

In London the news of the revolution came while the Fraternal Democrats were meeting. Thomas Frost, a young printer from Croydon, later recalled the moment:

Suddenly the news of the events in Paris was brought in. The effect was electrical. Frenchmen, Germans, Poles, Magyars sprang to their feet, embraced, shouted, gesticulated in the wildest enthusiasm. Snatches of oratory were delivered in excited tones, and flags were caught from the walls to be waved exultantly, amidst cries of 'Hoch!', 'Eljen!', 'Vive la République!' Then the doors were opened, and the whole assemblage descended to the street and, with linked arms and colours flying, marched to the meeting

---

15. Cooper, *Life*, p. 166.

place of the Westminster Chartists in Dean Street, Soho. There another enthusiastic fraternization took place, and great was the clinking of glasses that night in and around Soho and Leicester Square.[16]

The Chartist revival gathered strength in the excited weeks which followed. The National Petition contained at least 1.5 million signatures, and the gathering on Kennington Common to send it on its way to the House of Commons on 10 April was made up of tens of thousands. The Queen was despatched to the Isle of Wight. Soldiers were deployed in London in greater numbers than at any other time in the decade. There was certainly arming and drilling in some of the manufacturing districts. Ernest Jones and several of the London leaders were arrested and sentenced for seditious utterances. A conspiracy to effect a rising in London by a combined committee of Irish and Chartist leaders led to further arrests and deportations. In England, 1848 was certainly a turbulent year.[17]

It was not, however, a revolutionary year. The government never faltered – indeed seems only to have become seriously worried when there appeared to be some connection in Liverpool between Chartist and Irish dissidents. The middle class signed on as special constables, and the military stood by. If Chartism had ever represented a serious threat of armed rising it had been in 1839–40, when a rising did in fact occur in Newport and Chartists in some of the manufacturing districts prepared to take part in armed actions. In 1848 Chartism revived strongly in only some old centres, such as Yorkshire and Lancashire. It did not do so in South Wales, Nottingham, Birmingham or Leicester. Common cause was not established with Irish revolutionaries and, in any case, the nationalist movement on the island itself was weakened – both by the loss of its leaders and by the effects of the worst natural disaster to occur in nineteenth-century Europe.

---

16. T. Frost, *Forty Years' Recollections* (London, 1880), pp. 128–9.
17. D. Goodway, *London Chartism, 1838–1848* (Cambridge, 1982), pp. 68–96, 119–22, 129–49; Chase, *Chartism*, pp. 294–303, 312–26.

The Chartists put the admission of the workers to the franchise on the agenda. They also learned lessons about organization, which they used in the building-up of power bases in trade unions and other non-political forms of organization. Harney wrote in 1851: 'We are passing through another period of "reaction" – reaction in favour of social or rather industrial reform. The masses aspire to . . . accomplish the amelioration of their condition by means of labour associations, co-operative societies and trade unions.'[18] It was from these industrial and social bodies that working people were eventually to build and finance a political movement. One reason, incidentally, for the relegation to a lower order of priority of the panacea of manhood suffrage was the French experience, by which manhood suffrage resulted in the election of an emperor.

1848 was the end of a decade of mass pressure in Britain to open up the constitution to the excluded classes. The aim was not to overthrow the system, but to enlarge it. In most of Europe, 1848 saw revolts against old empires, usually all-class, nationalist revolts. The Chartists applauded, supported and celebrated these risings when it was in their power to do so. Ireland fitted the pattern of anti-imperial revolt, but famine, the secure and modern status of the British government, and the ambivalent attitudes to democratic reform at the heart of the nationalist movement, prevented the coming together of Irish nationalists in Ireland itself with the Chartists. The support for the repeal of the Act of Union, which came from the many Irish émigrés within the Chartist movement, never led to a combined assault on those in power in Britain during the 'year of revolutions'.

---

18.   *Friend of the People*, 18 January 1851.

14

THE BRITISH STATE
AND CHARTISM

JOHN SAVILLE, *1848: THE BRITISH STATE AND THE*
CHARTIST MOVEMENT (CAMBRIDGE, 1987)

John Saville locates the defeat of Chartism in the arena of
state repression and coercion.[1] This is one of the volume's
strengths: Saville has no difficulty in dealing with the
proposal that the state became 'liberalized' in its treatment
of working people in the late 1840s. The main purpose of
his study is to illustrate the toughness with which a confident bourgeoisie dealt with the challenge of Chartism in the
'year of revolutions'. He writes within a historiographical
tradition in which 1848 has been seen as a classic moment
of class confrontation, a trial of strength between (Chartist)
proletariat and (Whig) bourgeoisie, a moment invested
with a sense of failed revolution. By his title and by his use
of the Leninist notion of 'the state' as the main instrument
by which class power was maintained and defended, he
continues this tradition with little concern for a range of
alternative arguments.

   In his main argument Saville locates British domestic politics in 1848 within a 'triangle of revolutionary Paris,
insurgent Ireland and a revitalised native Chartist movement

---

1. This review first appeared in *History Workshop Journal* 28 (1989),
160–6. It is reproduced by permission of Oxford University Press. This
version has been slightly shortened.

in London and the industrial north'. The idea is attractive, but, if one takes a triangle as being three points which are connected, the connections are not really established. Indeed it could be argued that the three crucial nodes are themselves not clearly defined. There can be no argument about the effect which the February revolution had on the already reviving Chartist movement in some areas. But the revival was patchy and did not occur in all areas of former Chartist strength. The reasons for the discrepancies are not examined. Why did a revival take place in London and the West Riding and not in the great Chartist centres of Nottingham, Leicester, Birmingham or South Wales?

Already the triangle is a bit lopsided, since the areas of strong Chartist response undoubtedly overlap to a large extent with areas of large-scale Irish settlement. It is indeed suggested that the presence of a large number of Irish was a contributory factor in the revival in the areas under observation, but one would also need to know why other areas did not revive after the French revolution. There is a case for the argument that the presence of a large number of militant Irish in the areas of strong activity may actually have inhibited action in other districts. David Montgomery, in his examination of the contribution of different ethnic groups to the development of US trade unions, has suggested that people from predominantly Catholic areas in southern Europe were more difficult to enrol – their church discouraged union membership and their local traditions involved less structured labour organization. Once they had been recruited, however, they chafed under the northern European bureaucratic traditions and demanded more immediate and confrontational action.[2] It seems as though a somewhat similar situation may have affected the involvement of the Irish in Chartism. As J. H. Treble has shown, their church and their national leaders argued strongly against the involvement of Catholic Irishmen in British

---

2.   D. Montgomery, *The Fall of the House of Labor: The Workplace, the State and American Labor Activism, 1865–1925* (Cambridge, 1987).

political and labour organizations.[3] As I think I and John Belchem have demonstrated, such prohibitions had limited effects in the industrial districts – indeed Irishmen were among the outstanding local and national leaders of the radical movement.[4] It may have been the case, however, that the very nature of the break with traditional authority implied by an Irish Catholic's becoming involved in British politics put a heavier burden on him to look for immediate action. It also seems to have been the case that some at least of the Irishmen in the Chartist movement had already taken a stand on questions such as republicanism and the resort to armed revolt which had earned them forced exile from their own country, and to a degree estrangement from the mainstream of the nationalist movement there. A major weakness of Saville's analysis is that he makes very little reference to the politics of Irish nationalism. The question seems to him to be unproblematic – clearly the Irish were oppressed and exploited and so any action against British rule must have been part of an ideology of justified resistance. Unfortunately for Ireland – and for the aims of the nationalists and Chartists alike – the situation was never so straightforward.

Saville's 'triangle' never in fact existed as three points connected by any kind of common interest. That part of the second republic which could be seen as 'revolutionary' was gunned down in June – to the approval of John Mitchel, the Irish leader who appears most frequently in this volume as the voice of 'insurgent' Ireland. The politics of Paris, Ireland and England were not in phase in 1848. Ireland may indeed have been said to be 'insurgent' in 1843 when the last bluff of O'Connell's mass platform was called and a million people dispersed who might have attended the monster meeting at Clontarf. O'Connell, however, and his church, turned their backs on the escalation of the conflict to armed

---

3. J. H. Treble, 'O'Connor, O'Connell and the Attitudes of Irish Immigrants towards Chartism in the North of England, 1838–48', in J. Butt and I. F. Clark, eds, *The Victorians and Social Protest* (London, 1973).

4. J. Belchem, 'English Working-Class Radicalism and the Irish, 1815–1850', *North West Labour History Bulletin* 8 (1982/3).

rising, and, when Mitchel and the other Young Irelanders
finally broke with O'Connell and his heirs, they left themselves isolated from the mass of repealers. But even more
than the political disagreements of their leaders, the appall-
ing catastrophe of the famine, worsened in nearly all its
effects by the politics of relief (or non-relief) followed by
O'Connell's allies, the British Whigs, had left the Irish
people battered by disease, starvation and forced migration
and emigration. To describe them at that time as 'insurgent' is to make the word meaningless. What Saville refers
to as 'the abortive cabbage patch rising' demonstrated the
problems of arousing the country to active rebellion, as it
also demonstrated the isolation of the nationalist leaders.
The repeal movement had reached a high point under
O'Connell's leadership, when millions of ordinary men and
women supported it with money and with their physical
presence at meetings.

O'Connell was neither a republican nor a believer in
armed revolt, and the years of his reign saw the effective
crushing of the Jacobin and republican traditions in Ireland.
He claimed at his trial in 1844 that the Queen owed him a
particular debt of gratitude for his part in opposing
Chartism in Ireland and on the British mainland.[5] The
Confederates, returning belatedly to the tradition of the
United Irishmen in some respects, nevertheless refused
admission to the Dublin Chartists and rejected the six
points of the Charter as 'anathema'. The small, but not by
any means totally negligible, organization of Irish Catholics
gets no mention in this book, although their leader, the
Catholic wool merchant Patrick O'Higgins, was arrested
and imprisoned for sedition and the possession of arms in
1848. In Ireland itself the 'working compact between the
Irish nationalists and the English radicals that made 1848
such a promising year' can scarcely be said to have existed.
On the British mainland the compact existed at last in a

---

5.   *A Special Report of the Proceedings in the Case of the Queen against
Daniel O'Connell . . . on an Indictment for Conspiracy and Murder*
(Dublin, 1844), pp. 200–1, 376 and *passim*.

more formal way than hitherto, but it had little resonance
in Ireland and no effect on events in that country. Had the
breakthrough of Chartist/Jacobin ideas occurred in time to
influence policies in Ireland as it clearly did among the Irish
in Britain, the co-operation between the two movements
might have proved as dangerous as the British government
feared it would be.[6]

The 'triangle', then, is a notional one at best. The
February revolution in France proved to be a shot in the
arm to some Chartist localities, but why only some? What
had happened to Nottingham, Leicester, South Wales,
Birmingham? 1848 saw protest and activity in some
districts, particularly those of high Irish settlement, but we
still need to know why the general response was muted. It
still seems clear that the high point of Chartist activity was
in the 1838–40 period, and that the falling away needs to
be explained, since the evidence seems to suggest that there
was not a great change of heart about the need for the
inclusion of working people into the political system. The
arguments about the power of ideas, cosmologies, ideolo-
gies or whatever name may be used for belief systems are
extremely important, even for those of us who are not
prepared to explain the whole of history by the examination of one phenomenon. But nineteenth-century thought,
in all classes, was increasingly dominated by concepts based
on economics. Political change was losing its prophetic
power as the freeing of economic forces appeared to be
achieving results – whether through the repeal of the Corn
Laws or the achievement of wage negotiations – while the
arguments of socialists in France as well as in Britain turned
the ideas of many thoughtful working men away from politics and towards industrial and economic control.

An examination of the discussions and arguments among
Chartists in 1848 and after reveals some of the changes of
emphasis. At a delegate meeting of trades in March 1848,
some delegates argued that their problems were social
rather than political. A Chartist cabinetmaker responded

---

6.   T. Koseki, *1848: Chartism to Irish Nationalism* (Tokyo, 1993).

by appealing to the experience of France: 'Almost the first act of the provincial government was to look to the interest of labour (loud cheers). The French people were promised a Minister of Industry (cheers) – but why? Because universal suffrage now prevailed in that country (loud cheers)'.[7] This is the language of Social Democracy, or of Jacobinism. It was the language of the working class in the sense that it probably, by 1848, represented the aspirations of the majority of Chartists. In the Marxist sense, if the working class only expresses its 'true' consciousness if it proposes the expropriation of capital and the overthrow of the bourgeois state, there is little evidence of such consciousness to be found in 1848. It should, moreover, be remembered that fifteen years of radical activity in the manufacturing districts had brought into being self-help organizations: Sunday schools, Land Company branches, co-operative societies, mechanics' institutes and other bodies which had, to some extent, provided means of escape for the better-off working-class families as well as providing a vested interest in peaceful industrial relations and municipal development.

John Saville is not, of course, unaware of these developments, though he may underestimate their importance as influences on thought and action. There is, however, an implication in much of what he writes, as there is in the work of some other more theoretical writers, that 'armed resistance' was simply one item on a menu of possible tactics to be employed by radical or nationalist movements. In fact, of course, a recourse to arms meant abandoning work, home and family, and the possible – indeed probable – loss of life in fighting or as punishment. Men rarely follow leaders advocating armed rebellion unless they have nothing to lose or unless they are fairly certain of victory. For the Chartists, as for the Irish, recent history offered little hope. 1798 had seen the butchery of rebellious Irishmen by trained British troops, but also the commission of sectarian atrocities and the isolation and destruction of

---

7. *Northern Star*, 25 March 1848, cited in J. Belchem, 'Chartism and the Trades, 1848–49', in *English Historical Review* XCVIII (1983).

the nation's leaders. 1839 in Wales had shown the effectiveness of a small body of trained troops against an army of determined but untrained and under-equipped working men. Saville states that 'a tradition of insurrection had not been established on the British mainland', and suggests that 'if there had been a coherent leadership, whether open or underground, it is likely the Irish would have followed since repeal was an avowed aim of the Chartist movement.' But what is a 'tradition of insurrection', and how might one have been 'established'? The Chartists in 1838–39 had a strong rhetoric of defensive preparation – 'If they Peterloo us, we'll Moscow them' – but proposals for armed action of an organized kind, apart from defence against government terror, seem to have rested mainly with small metropolitan Jacobin groups or with proposals for the rescue of the condemned Welsh leaders which were defused by the commutation of the death sentences. Even Daniel O'Connell, with his declared unwillingness to shed a drop of human blood, was not averse to using lines about 'fleshing every sword to the hilt', but, like Feargus O'Connor, he relied on the pressure of the mass, open, constitutional platform and the demand for political rights – an Irish Parliament or manhood suffrage, based on a demonstration of the numbers who demanded it. The extent to which such a platform agitation necessarily contained the threat of further action if its demands were refused or if its leaders were attacked is one of the problems which historians of mass popular movements have to examine in particular circumstances. It may have been that the threat of armed uprising by the Chartists was greater in 1848 than in 1839, but I very much doubt it. Had the authorities attacked any of the monster meetings of the summer of 1838 or 1839 one can envisage a national response of the kind which formed the Newport Rising. By 1848 the element of fear of an all-out offensive on the institutions and communities of working people which had been present in many parts of the country in 1838–39, and the sense of being under constant threat of attack, had gone. As Harney recalled many years later, speaking of the autumn of 1839:

> One marked feature . . . had been the consensus of opinion
> that force would have to be resorted to to obtain justice and
> the acknowledgement of right . . . it was not only Dr Taylor
> and others in unison with his view who referred to the
> probable employment of force, but also those who, at least
> later, acquired a character for moderation, who held the
> same view and expressed themselves in like terms.[8]

By 1846, Harney was warning Engels that there was very
little likelihood that the British people would ever take up
arms to achieve change.[9]

What, then, do we learn about 1848 from this book?
That the British state – taken to include the government,
military, police, magistracy and judiciary – was better
prepared to put down radical activity in 1848 than had
been the case a decade earlier. Policing in Britain and
Ireland was more widespread and more efficient, although
it would have been interesting to know more about the
direct relationship between the policing in the two areas –
what elements of the Irish experience sharpened the tools
which were used in mainland Britain, and what elements
were considered too draconian or too potentially inflam-
matory to be used in any but a colonial situation. Juries
were packed in Ireland, where a single Catholic juryman
caused the authorities some problems in earlier trials and
where John Mitchel believed he would have been better
served had he not been tried by a jury of fellow Protestants.
To some extent, as the Chartists continually pointed out,
the property qualifications for British juries ensured a
ready-packed jury for all trials of Chartists and other working people, an argument with which John Mitchel had little
sympathy. He commented on the conviction of Ernest Jones
and his fellow Chartists in 1848 that, 'If juries were not
packed, they have nothing to complain of; if they were
fairly tried by their fellow countrymen and found guilty,
why they are guilty.'

---

8. *Newcastle Weekly Chronicle*, 5 January 1890.
9. F. G. and R. M. Black, *The Harney Papers* (Assen, 1969), p. 240.

To the question of why Chartism, in spite of the stimulus of the February revolution, the horrors of famine and oppression in Ireland and the high level of political awareness and literacy among the working population of Britain, declined rapidly after the events of the summer of 1848 and indeed had been declining in many hitherto strong areas, the book offers little in the way of new theories. It refutes some of the superficial arguments of linguistic analysts, but provides no very convincing new suggestions.

Neither the efficiency of the state nor the resilience of the economy gives a sufficient answer to why, for instance, there was almost no political agitation in the bitter winter of 1855. The answer to the question of why working people lost their passionate faith in the efficacy of political action has to be found partly by the examination of changes in ideas and perceptions, as well as in the experience of the Chartists and ex-Chartists.

From the ideology of free trade and laissez-faire economics through the spectrum to the socialist panacea of the abolition of private property, the old Jacobin/Paineite arguments for political participation, individual freedom in property, labour and belief within a liberal legal framework had taken a beating. Convinced Chartists reverted to the 'No Politics' rule in their trade societies, and co-operators and trade unionists looked to organizational self-help rather than to government intervention. Was this change in perspective, though, the only reason for the many changes in the activities of former radicals? Why were the radical women so conspicuously absent from later Chartist politics and from the co-ops and friendly societies of the post-Chartist years? There is a lot more to be discovered by an examination of 1848.

15

THE POST-CHARTIST DECADES

MARGOT C. FINN, *AFTER CHARTISM: CLASS
AND NATION IN ENGLISH RADICAL POLITICS
1848–1874* (CAMBRIDGE, 1993)

MILES TAYLOR, *THE DECLINE OF BRITISH
RADICALISM 1847–1860* (OXFORD, 1995)

Historians of popular culture and popular movements have
always had particular problems in dealing with rhetoric and
vocabulary.[1] The written record in the hands of largely
middle-class scribes has dictated the meaning of such terms
as 'democracy', while the resonances of the platform and
the mass demonstration have gone for ever. An example of
this is the idea of annual parliaments, long written off as 'a
mistake' in the Chartist political programme without a serious consideration of the alternative kind of crowd politics
which such a proposal implied. The modern revival of the
political referendum may perhaps raise again some of the
concepts of the interaction between elected members and
the individual voter which were contained in the idea of
annual parliaments. But the discussion about the franchise
after the Chartists was carried out within the discourse of
what Carlyle called the 'talking classes', and was concerned
almost exclusively with what the sage contemptuously

---

1. This essay is made up of two reviews published in the *Times Literary
Supplement*, 14 January 1994 and the *Times Higher Education Supplement*,
22 September 1995. Both reviews have been slightly shortened.

described as 'one's right to vote for the Member of Parliament, to send one's twenty-thousandth part of a master of tongue-fence to National Palaver'.[2] By 1867 former Chartists and sections of their erstwhile middle-class opponents united to welcome the admission of male urban artisans to the franchise. Margot Finn's book looks at some of the conflicts and realignments which took place among radicals between 1848 and the Reform Act of 1867.

As long ago as 1927 Frances Elma Gillespie published her pioneering study of the radical, liberal and labour politics of the post-Chartist decades.[3] She demonstrated the effect which a decade of highly-charged popular crowd politics had wrought on the mainstream politics of Britain, and in particular looked in some detail at the attempts by a series of radical political and social movements to come to terms with, co-opt or contest the firm assertion of the working man's place in politics which she saw as the main legacy of Chartism. Her work has been under-used since its publication, either because subsequent accounts of the movement have tended to assume a simple 'economic recovery' explanation for the fading militancy of the post-Chartist years or because other explanatory theses were advanced which did not require a close examination of the publications or the politics of those years. Theses such as the 'labour aristocracy' theory, by which skilled workmen were seen to have been bought off with the spoils of high Victorian imperialism, or the theory of the victory of the 'entrepreneurial ideal', by which the articulate workmen were converted to a belief in the free market and free trade as the road to social achievement and eventual political enfranchisement, or the proposition that the Chartists were trapped by a purely political programme into believing that they had won their battle when political liberalism took over from the confrontational politics of the Chartist decades, did not require much in the way of detailed examination of the

---

2. Carlyle, *Chartism*, p. 55.
3. F. E. Gillespie, *Labor and Politics in England, 1850–1867* (Durham, N.C., 1927).

confused political groupings and regroupings among the ex-Chartists and ultra-radical and dissenting members of the middle class.

In a densely written examination of the post-Chartist decades, Margot Finn has gone back to the period and produced a descriptive and, to some extent, an analytical account of the changing organizational forms and of the overarching principles which informed them. In particular she contests those interpretations which have claimed that nationalism replaced class consciousness, and that this made easier the coming-together of the social democratic beliefs of middle-class Liberals. Her argument here is completely convincing as far as it goes. Outstanding is a brilliant second chapter which traces an English radical tradition in which civil and religious liberty are closely associated with national independence in a pan-European world-view. She has no problem in demonstrating the power of the European nationalist movements as inspirational examples to the late Chartists, or in showing that, far from displacing class loyalties, such moments as Garibaldi's visit to Britain in 1864 actually precipitated domestic political programmes based on class loyalty and the revival of the demand for manhood suffrage. Her account of the Garibaldi episode is one of the best we have, and forms a valuable chapter in the confused political discussion of the period.

There are nevertheless problems with Finn's argument. Like 'democracy', 'nationalism' has layers of meaning. Historians who have seen nationalism as displacing class feelings have often meant not the heroic secular nationalism of the European nation state, but the more complex and often contradictory nationalism of a nation whose growing world influence and wealth was based partly on the exploitation of colonial territories. While the old Chartists and their radical-liberal allies were welcoming Garibaldi and raising money to send forces to his aid, many of the Irish were parading in support of the Pope and attacking the supporters of the Italian patriot. Finn's account of these decades does not look at the ethnic conflicts in Lancashire, where class and national rhetoric became more complex. The nationalism of 1848 was, after all, aimed against authoritarian government. In the same way, an account of the years 1848–74 which makes no mention of the Indian uprising of 1857 must inevitably ignore divisions among radicals which are less easy to define in class terms. Ernest Jones stood firmly in support of the 'revolt of Hindostan'; he also supported Irish nationalism and defended in court the Fenians charged with the murder of Sergeant Brett in 1867.[4] This support by Jones and other members of the Reform League for the Fenians led to the resignation of middle-class members from its council and was, as Antony Taylor has demonstrated, one of the points with which Manchester Liberals found it difficult to come to terms when Jones joined their ranks after the 1867 Reform Act.[5] But by no means all the well-known former Chartists recognized the nationalism of the Irish peasant or the Sepoy warrior as on a par with that of Garibaldi.

Another aspect of nationalism which is skated over by Finn is the power of monarchism. She does describe an interesting episode in which protests at Victoria's effusive greeting of the French emperor were accompanied by expressions of loyalty and respect for the Queen herself – something which would hardly have been found in radical comment during the Chartist years. The growth among working people of a personal loyalty to Victoria seems to have been demonstrated dramatically by the failure of the short-lived republican impulse of the late 1860s, and may indeed be interpreted as a reinforcing element in one kind of cross-class nationalism. Finn, in short, makes her case with respect to the secular national movements of Europe and shows that support for these by and large encouraged working-class reform movements in England, but she leaves unanswered more complex questions of national identity

---

4. Taylor, *Ernest Jones*, pp. 227–31.
5. A. Taylor, 'The Best Way to Get What He Wanted: Ernest Jones and the Boundaries of Liberalism in the Manchester Election of 1868', in *Parliamentary History* 16 (1997), 185–204.

and racial and ethnic attitudes which were also of importance in forming the leaders and supporters of the popular movements which emerged from the political melting pot of the post-Chartist decades.

The Decline of British Radicalism, 1847–1860 is clearly the outcome of an industriously pursued doctoral thesis, but topped up, the author informs us, by the incorporation of the insights of the 'linguistic turn' in historiography. Alas, like so much of the material emanating from that particular stable, the first problem we encounter is one of clarification and definition of terms. It seems impossible that anyone could take the term 'radical' as unproblematic, but we are in fact never offered a definition of its use in the book. Even more oddly, the core of the book is an examination of a so-called Reform Party in Parliament. It is never explained quite what definition of the very political term 'party' may be held to include O'Connor, Cobden, Bright, William Williams and a disparate group from both sides of the House of Commons and from none, many of whom were barely on speaking terms with each other.[6] It seems in fact to be a term used to avoid clear definition rather than aid it.

The main thesis of my book on Chartism is that the reform agitation in the 1830s and particularly the activity in Parliament of the 'radicals' who were responsible for the 1834 Poor Law Amendment Act, the 1835 Municipal Corporations Act, the 1839 Rural Police Act and other root-and-branch 'reforms', together with the extra-parliamentary activity of the magistracy and the judiciary, especially in the 1834 Tolpuddle labourers and the 1837 Glasgow cotton spinners' episodes, turned the popular mind towards access to law-making and parliamentary reform as a method of dealing with their problems.

Anyone who has followed the post-Chartist lives of the local figures will see that the great majority moved back, during the 1840s, to the organization of trades, friendly

---

6. For Williams, see S. Roberts in *The House of Commons, 1832–1868* (forthcoming).

societies and co-operative organizations. Very many emigrated to the United States or to the Antipodes.[7] A few remained at the fringes of conventional politics as temperance lecturers and local councillors, mostly at the popular end of Liberal politics, which began to seek the artisan and small-business vote during the years of Tory government in the mid-1840s. These latter are the people Miles Taylor takes as in some way typifying the ex-Chartists, although Margot Finn in her much more closely textured work on one aspect of post-Chartist politics – nationalism – has shown other areas of concern on the part of that small minority of Chartist activists who remained linked with British and European politics. But the point about the ex-Chartists was that they retreated from national and to a great extent from local politics into other more local and, in some ways, much narrower and less ideological forms of activity. When a new political labour movement arose, four decades after the end of Chartism, it arose from these 'non-political' forms of labour organization and not from some 'radical' enclave within the parliamentary Liberal Party.

The Chartist movement had a necessarily short life as a mass movement. Poor people's movements do not have the resources to sustain a permanent organization; they gain their effect in particular short-term ways. The Chartist movement had many effects, and in many ways changed the terms of nineteenth-century politics. For all the divisions and tensions within it, it did bring a whole new class into the political map of the nation. But its influences were, like all political forms throughout the major part of the nineteenth century, at least as much provincial as national

---

7. Not all those Chartists who emigrated to America stayed there: the London activist John Alexander (1808–72) was soon disillusioned and returned after less than a year. However, John Campbell (1810–74), the secretary of the NCA, settled in Philadelphia, making a living as a bookseller and a journalist; John Cluer (1806–86) of Glasgow and John Hinchcliffe (1806–67) of Bradford became leading figures in US trade unions. See C. Godfrey, *Chartist Lives*, pp. 440, 472–3, 487, 507–8. George Binns emigrated to New Zealand in 1842: his story is told in Roberts, *Radical Politicians and Poets*, pp. 39–57.

and they simply cannot be understood by an analysis of the parliamentary division lists. Outside periods of national emergency, in particular the emergency of a major war and its aftermath, the political powers that affected the common people of Britain during the nineteenth century were the still-powerful figures of the employer, the landlord, the magistrate and, to some extent, the priest: it was precisely the retreat from the centralizing politics of the radical reformers of the 1830s, exemplified by the 1847 modification of the Poor Law and the slow and cautious introduction of policing nationally, that made it possible for regularly employed working people to return to their own forms of protection and defence within their own trades and their own communities. To see such activities as 'non-political' is to use a very narrow definition of politics.

Taylor's book is part of a move from a historiography too heavily weighted towards the economic and social back to a concern with the history of politics and political ideas. Most social historians welcome the change of emphasis, but the new political history must surely take account of new questions posed of old political concepts by the more recent disciplines, and not simply return unproblematically to the old nineteenth-century political terminology.

V

LOOKING BACK

This collection concludes, very appropriately, with Thompson's reflections, late in her life, on how Marxist ideas shaped her thinking both as a political activist and as an historian. She concludes that a rigid adherence to Marxist theory only leads to a misunderstanding of what the Chartists achieved. These remarks were made at the launch of John Saville's *Memoirs from the Left* in 2003.

16

REFLECTIONS ON
MARXIST TELEOLOGY

With the death of Michel Fuchs we have lost a friend whose work and whose company was a constant pleasure and a constant challenge.[1] He was an ideas man and a language man. Although he and I were for most of the time a continent apart, by email and by telephone I valued his company and his wit and wisdom on questions of language, literature and history in the fields of work that we shared. I no longer do much research and don't have any up-to-date original research to offer to his memorial volume. Instead here is a short piece based on the transcript of a contribution I made to the meeting to launch the memoirs of my old friend Professor John Saville of the University of Hull. I had gladly agreed to take part in the book launch, but, when I was sent the invitation, I found the organizers had rearranged things and had called the event 'Marxism and History', with Eric Hobsbawm, John himself and me listed as speakers. Eric has a lifelong commitment to Marxism and history and would, I knew, make a serious and considered contribution on the subject. If I had tried to give a talk with the same subject matter I would, at best, have been repeating what he would already have presented in a much

---

1. This essay was first published in *Cycnos* 24 (2007), 155–60.

better form. So my contribution was perhaps a little less serious than it might otherwise have been, but it nevertheless touches on some of the problems with which I have been concerned during seventy-odd years as an historian and political activist.

I want to start with my friend Ali. I live in Worcester, a cathedral city which is on the whole fairly prosperous and pleasant. I live in the most working-class area and Ali is the man who keeps the newspaper shop. He is a good friend. He helps run and organize a credit union that we are trying to get off the ground and so, as well as buying newspapers from him, I work with him in the credit union. His family comes from Kashmir, but, as he speaks English with a strong West Midlands accent, I imagine he came over when he was very young. He does, though, keep in touch with his family and is very much in touch with the subcontinent in general. I have learnt a lot from him. When I have been in his shop and heard him arguing with customers, he has always been arguing and explaining about the politics of the Far East in ways to which I find myself sympathetic and with which I usually agree. When the other customers have gone, we sometimes talk about politics, about the Afghan war and other things which concern him and me and our city.

One day we had been talking about politics and Ali said, 'What do you think is going to happen?' That is not an easy question to answer and I just said, 'Well, I don't think things are going to get much better.' He said (and I have probably got the details wrong here because I didn't note it down) words to the effect that 'the prophet will come back to the world and he will live for a time and he will have a son and after that everything will be alright. It says so in the holy books and that is what I believe.' I walked home absolutely staggered. Week after week, day after day, I had been discussing politics with this very knowledgeable, rational and reasonable chap who, in the end, believed that a pre-existing programme coming from outside the world would intervene in the affairs of the world and ensure a promised outcome.

But I have to admit that, as I thought about this, I had a sense of déjà vu. Last week I was at a socialist history seminar in this city and one of the comrades said, as if it were en passant, 'Of course, the working class will transform the world', and I realized where my sense of déjà vu came from. Everything Eric says about the fear of Marxism, and the power of it when we were younger, is obviously true and he is a much more serious person than I am. Nevertheless, underlying so many activities, the writing and the theorizing, has been this teleological pattern – primitive communism, feudalism, transition from feudalism to capitalism, capitalism and finally socialism. These changes of system are to occur by violent revolutions and once the final one to produce socialism has occurred, the class struggle will be ended. The prehistory of class-riven society will pass and the real struggle of man against the environment will begin. This is, of course, a simplification, but nevertheless, if we look at a great deal of the writing about popular history that has been done in our lifetimes, we see some of the problems that this teleology has brought to the subject. I have to confess that I came to the study of history by way of literature and language, and not by way of the 'science' of economics as the other two contributors did. Economics has never quite had the prescriptive power for me that it has for some and I have always viewed it with some suspicion. I accept it when it describes things; I have problems when it predicts things, and this may well have affected my approach to history.

When you get old – into the eighties – you tend to think that all the golden things happened in your youth. I do think, nevertheless, that the years following the Second World War saw a huge explosion of intellectual activity. History, literature, sociology and other social sciences saw fundamental changes of direction. People like Richard Hoggart and Raymond Williams, as well as the members of the Communist Party Historians' Group and many social scientists, were much more concerned with the people of the country than with its institutions, its bloodlines and its high politics. Even economic history departments tacked 'and social' on to their titles and introduced labour history into the syllabus. I think this is partly because many of the academics were, or had been, communists and had developed their interest in the common people – at least in the male ones – through their wartime experiences in the forces and in industry. This is where we all were in our teens and twenties. We were learning that ordinary people were often more able than we were. They brought to the business of fighting a war, at all the different levels, abilities which those of us who had had sheltered upbringings and had gone to rather posh schools had never really met. Working with people of all classes, at all levels of authority, reinforced our socialism and diminished any hesitance we might have had in embracing the revolutionary values of liberty, fraternity and equality. I think it was this wartime experience, both as civilians and as service men and women, that aroused the great interest in history in the second half of the last century, in ways which were exploratory and, in some ways, explosive.

Labour history was not new. Douglas Cole, Lance Beales and a few others had already mapped out some of the territory, but our generation has brought to it another experience and this affected our work and our politics in good and bad ways.[2] In good ways, the Communist Party was a great organizing body. It really got things done. Members gave up all kinds of private and social activity in order to concentrate on the political task and they got on with it. On the other hand, it did cut us off from a great deal of the radical political activity that was informing the whole population. Everybody else who had served in the war had shared this experience of defeating one of the most evil dictatorships that had ever existed and starting to build a new world. But many of us – because we were so sure that only Marxists had the true prescription for the transformation of

---

2. G. D. H. Cole, *A Short History of the British Working-Class Movement* (London, 1925–27); G. D. H. Cole and R. Postgate, *The Common People* (London, 1938) and H. L. Beales, *The Early English Socialists* (London, 1933).

society – were not prepared to accept lesser transformations. One of the first arguments I had in print was on the question of 'palliatives'.

There is a revolutionary tradition in British politics dating at least from the second half of the nineteenth century which claims that reforms introduced by reactionary governments, conservative or social-democratic, make the people more satisfied with capitalist society and therefore hold back the essential socialist revolution. Free education, trade-union recognition and free or subsidized health services seduce some sections of the working class and thus delay the essential defeat of capitalism. Some Communist Party members therefore did not welcome the Beveridge Report, or the setting up of the National Health Service and the post-1944 education system. Others of us felt that whatever the danger of palliatives, these welfare state moves did embody some of the values that had made us socialists. Now, in the various battles to defend the principles of the health and education and other services, we can see that they were far from being palliative in effect, but were important ways in which socialist values have been to a degree incorporated in modern society. In the past we were often so sure that we had the only answer to the creation of a just society that we were prepared to cut corners and use any method to make revolutionary changes. 'Truth', as one party organizer told me when I was in the Young Communist League, 'is what helps in the class struggle.' As well as making the communists objects of mistrust among the general public – people to be voted for in tough trade-union situations but rarely in local or national politics – this attitude made us lose respect for the important utopian traditions in British socialist thought. The division made between 'utopian' and 'scientific' socialism narrowed the spectrum of the study of radical and labour history. The great utopias have been treated as though they were models for post-revolutionary societies and not sites for social criticism.

In our writing of labour and social history, we have also been to a degree entrapped in the teleology of Marxist analysis. We looked back for signs of revolutionary change and saw Chartism, for example, as a failed revolution. We applied the same template to most European societies, though we had problems when it came to Asia so tended to look at countries there simply as victims of European imperialism. In looking at European societies through the teleological lens we saw that popular movements which failed to rise and destroy the capitalist system were either premature or inadequately led.

My main interest has always been in the Chartist Movement, and, when I first came to it, much of the Marxist history was written within this teleology. The Chartist leaders, by their timidity or conservatism, had let down the class-conscious and revolutionary British crowd, had drawn back just at the moment when armed revolution was possible. That there were genuine revolutionaries among the leadership was clear. We remember Theodore Rothstein's discovery of George Julian Harney; Bolshevik Bronterre O'Brien has also been a candidate for revolutionary leader, as have some less well-known figures.[3] The actual leaders, Feargus O'Connor in particular, were regarded as backward-looking or cowardly. Discussion about the class make-up of Chartism and its ideas has almost always been based on the theory that 'real' working-class movements must be based on a programme of the expropriation of the expropriators, and that anything short of that was merely an extension of the bourgeois ideas of democracy. In fact these historians were more concerned with what the working class of the period ought to have been doing than what it was actually doing. Many aspects of Chartism, the Land Company to name but one, were sidelined because they did not fit the revolutionary pattern. Since it was always assumed that heightened class consciousness, once achieved, had lifted labour politics on to a higher level, the problem remained that the unified class feelings of the first half of the century clearly lessened, at least in their revolutionary potential, after the mid-century. The theory

---

3. T. Rothstein, *From Chartism to Labourism* (London, 1929).

of the 'labour aristocracy' came to the rescue here – with the suggestion that the better-off skilled workers were bought off by the bourgeoisie with the wealth gained from imperial expansion. What the Chartists pulled off in terms of experience – the modification of many of the most brutal and confrontational actions of the post-1832 governments and, above all, the foundation of sources of social and political power in the form of national trade unions, co-operative societies, building societies and other bases from which working-class political structures were to emerge – were rarely considered as Chartist achievements.

So, when condemning revolutionary failures, labour historians often overlooked considerable achievements. They also failed to record activity which did not fit the pattern. I was originally disappointed at the limited demand for female suffrage and other items of the later feminist agendas. Although there were plenty of women in evidence, they seemed, for the most part, happy to demand the vote for their husbands and brothers, and never asked for the right to work. When, in 1968 or so, I gave a talk on Chartist women in New York, the first question I was asked was, 'Did Chartist women demand twenty-four-hour child care?' I had to explain to the radical feminist who asked it that what Chartist women wanted for the most part was the chance to stay at home and mind their children instead of working in a mill, to be allowed to receive poor relief in their homes and not to hand their children over to the Poor Law authorities and, above all, for their husbands to receive a wage that would enable them to bring up families in reasonable comfort, without their or their children's need to go out to work. If they should have been asking for a share in the productive process, for the most part they certainly were not.

What I have been trying to say is that the teleological element in Marxist thought and analysis has too often distorted the way we look at history – and indeed the way we look at contemporary events, particularly in some of the post-colonial countries. This does not deny the many insights into history and politics that reading Marx has given me and most of our generation. Edward, my husband, used to say that he worked within a Marxist tradition, and I would say the same. There are many problems with the tradition – for Edward it was always the same concern with morality, even with a definition of the moral dimension in society. At a simpler level, it is the danger of approaching historical events with a ready-made test kit, derived from any kind of holy writ.

What is left of Marx if you abandon the teleology? Well, Marx himself welcomed *On the Origin of Species* (1859) and the theory of evolution because it offered the possibility of progress without teleology. It is perhaps unfair to label his sophisticated analysis 'teleology', but it is nevertheless based on an accepted view of past historical development which dictates what are the essential questions for historians to examine. We could say that it is not absolutely teleographic because it ends up by saying that society has to achieve the best way to survive on the planet, and, even within its own theory, this does not have to be socialism; but still he and Engels thought it was.

I don't call myself a Marxist – and nor did Edward.[4] On the Latin American question, there are surely moments there when we are looking at the struggle of the poor against the rich, not a struggle between classes standing in differing relations to the means of production. It was Marx's great achievement to describe class conflict within many societies, but many of us would not give the absolute priority to economic relations which he undoubtedly did, or assume its near-universality. The terms of much Marxist and Marxist historiography limit historical research: judgemental terms such as 'backward-looking' applied to agricultural or societal systems do not help objective analysis. As an example, a now well-known scholar once argued with me that child labour in the factories was a good thing because it hastened the development of mature capitalism, without which socialism could not develop!

---

4. When I asked Edward, in 1991, if he still described himself as a Marxist, he replied without hesitation that he preferred to call himself 'a Morrisist'.

FURTHER READING

Out-of-print for many years, a new edition of Dorothy Thompson's *The Chartists* was released in 2013. Her *Outsiders: Class, Gender and Nation* (London, 1993) has, in its six essays, a lot to say about Chartism. I would also like to draw attention to the introduction Thompson contributed to Owen Ashton, Robert Fyson and Stephen Roberts, eds, *The Chartist Movement: A New Annotated Bibliography* (London, 1995). It does not say anything Thompson had not said before, but it is a concise expression of her views and should not be overlooked. Despite the no-more-than-satisfactory quality of a few of the illustrations, Stephen Roberts and Dorothy Thompson, eds, *Images of Chartism* (Rendlesham, 1998) filled a gap that had, surprisingly, existed until then.

Thompson welcomed the appearance of Malcolm Chase, *Chartism: A New History* (Manchester, 2007), and it does indeed provide the reliable, richly detailed, and fair-minded single-volume narrative history of the movement that was badly needed. Richard Brown, *Chartism: Rise and Demise* (Dunstable, 2014) is a very thorough survey based on wide reading. Feargus O'Connor has finally found his biographer – Paul A. Pickering, *Feargus O'Connor* (Monmouth, 2008) is excellent. In another impressive book, *Ernest*

Jones, Chartism and the Romance of Politics (Oxford, 2003), Miles Taylor casts a sceptical but nevertheless fair eye over the career of this most popular of popular leaders. Stephen Roberts, *The Chartist Prisoners* (Oxford, 2008) tells the stories of Thomas Cooper and Arthur O'Neill who, after sharing a prison cell, formed a friendship that lasted fifty years. David Goodway, *George Julian Harney: The Chartists Were Right* (London, 2014) reprints a selection of his late journalism and is warmly recommended. If proof were needed that local investigations of Chartism still have value, then it is to be found in Robert G. Hall's fine study of Ashton-under-Lyne – *Voices of the People: Democracy and Chartist Political Identity, 1830–1870* (Monmouth, 2007). Finally, two special issues of *Labour History Review* (London, 2009 and 2013), edited by Joan Allen and Owen R. Ashton, bring together some of the papers presented at Chartism Days – themselves legacies of Thompson's belief that, collaboratively, we can rediscover and remember the achievements of the Chartists.

INDEX